ARMAGH ROAD PRESBYTERIAN CHURCH

PORTADOWN

1868 - 2009

BY MERVYN D. GILMOUR

2009

Published by Armagh Road Presbyterian Church, Portadown

Foreword

In following the Author of this book as Clerk of Session I feel privileged to be asked to write an introduction to Mervyn's re-writing and update of his previous history of Armagh Road Presbyterian Church - "100 not out". This small book recorded the important events and people in the life of the Church from its foundation in 1868 through to 1968 and is now updated to 2009.

Armagh Road Church has been first and foremost, a place of worship, Sunday by Sunday, for well over 100 years. The purpose - to Glorify God - is unchanged and unchanging. The Church is a pleasant building which most of us, whether we grew up in it or not, have grown to love and just sitting in it can often help us to be still and open to God's presence.

Mervyn Gilmour

History, and particularly the history of the Presbyterian Church, is a subject which has interested Mervyn for many years - being a member of the Presbyterian Historical Society and past assistant secretary of same - he has carried that level of knowledge and interest through into the current book.

Mervyn omits to mention that he has been an elder in the Presbyterian Church for 50 years and has served as clerk of session with distinction, quiet dignity, wise council and dry humour - some of which is apparent in the text. Our thanks are extended to Mervyn for taking the time and making the effort to bring us up to date.

The Rev W. S. Magee, in the postscript to the previous history, suggested that the church had been built on the devotion of its people and on their willingness to spend and to be spent but warned of complacency and suggested then as now that "Our future rests in God's gracious will". This was true in 1968 and is still true today.

May I commend this book to you in that our future as a Church is built on our past - without yesterday's parents, tomorrow's children will have no opportunity to build on the past 140 years.

Ivan Stirling
Clerk of Session

Presbyterianism in Portadown

Portadown, and its churches, grew up in the nineteenth century. In the eighteenth century Portadown was just a village, smaller than Tandragee, and without any churches.

While there were no churches in the town, worshippers attended the Presbyterian Church at Vinecash (the oldest Presbyterian Church in the area), and the Church of Ireland Churches at Drumcree and Seagoe.

The latter was a particularly well-endowed church, and a visitor in 1813 wrote, apparently quite seriously, about the rector's carriage, "I was much edified at seeing the great splendour of this Gospel minister so far superior to any of his auditors".

John Wesley visited the area in 1767 and made his famous remark that Portadown was "a place not much troubled with any kind of religion"; and perhaps for that reason he made several further visits. He built up a strong group of Methodists, and the first church to be built in Portadown was a Methodist one, somewhere between Church Lane and Mandeville Street, in 1802. St. Mark's Church of Ireland Church (at first called St. Martin's) was built in 1826.

In the nineteenth century, Portadown began to grow. A canal system linked up with rivers meant that Portadown really was a port, with boats coming from Newry on the way to Lough Neagh and the centre of Ulster. The town was an important market for linen and grain. When the railway from Belfast reached Portadown in 1842, and when that railway

Vinecash Presbyterian, founded 1697

The first Church of the Presbyterians in Portadown, built 1822

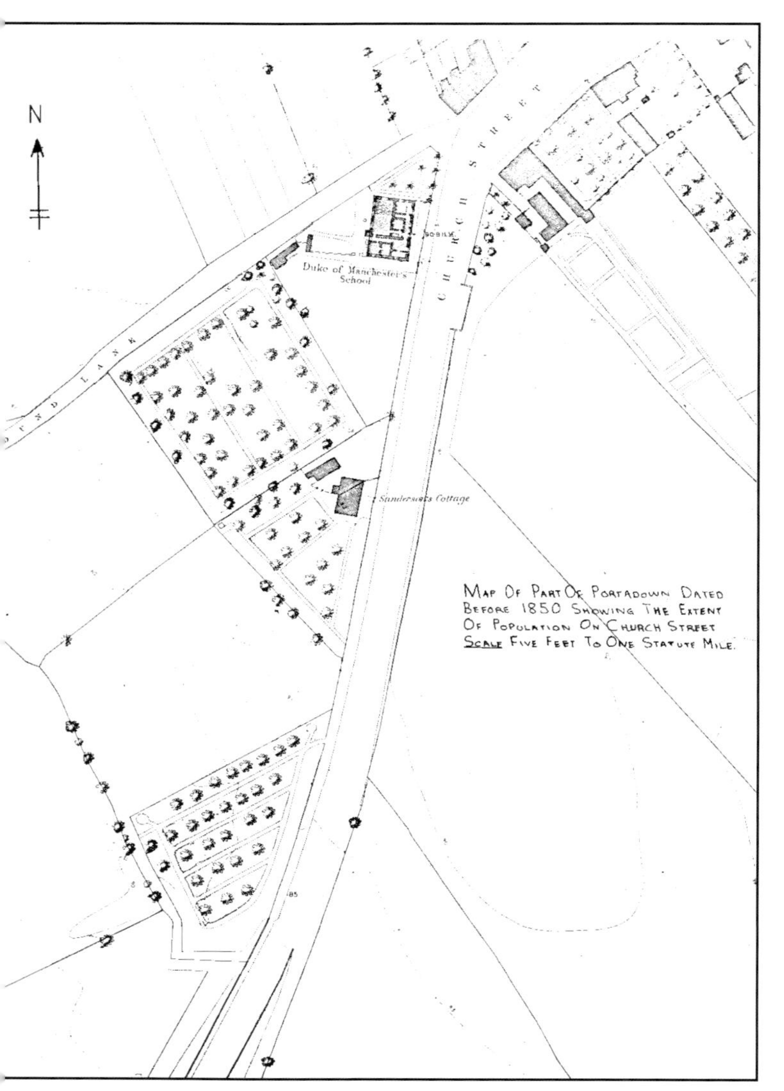

Map of Portadown Church Street Area, 1850

Edenderry Presbyterian Church, 1922

was extended to Armagh in 1848 and to Dublin in 1855, Portadown could claim to be "the hub of the North", and the town grew rapidly. The population, which was under 1,000 in 1820, became 2,500 in 1841 and 5,500 by 1861.

Presbyterians, who had been meeting in the basement of a house where the Ulster Bank now stands, opened the first Portadown Presbyterian Church (Edenderry) in 1822, on the site of the present Edenderry Church's lecture hall. As the number of Presbyterians grew, the present Edenderry Church building was opened in 1857. (Its transepts, gallery and organ were added later.)

Formation of the Second Presbyterian Congregation

There seem to be two reasons why, around the year 1865, a new Presbyterian Church was required. One was the growth in population; the other was the effect of the 1859 Revival.

In 1866 the citizens of Portadown organised a petition, asking that Portadown be made a Parliamentary seat. In it they claimed that the growth in population, from 820 in 1820 to 7,000 in 1866, was the largest percentage increase in Ireland. Even though these figures seem to be a little inflated, there is no doubt that Portadown was expanding at an extraordinary rate, and that one minister must have found it difficult to cope with the influx.

The Religious Revival of 1859, a movement in which, as the historian of First Portadown Church writes, “men and women were swept into the Kingdom of grace as by a mighty rushing wind”, had an enormous effect on church life. One of the historians of the movement, Dr Orr, estimates that through it the Irish Presbyterian Church received over 60,000 converts in the years 1859-61. One of the many results of all this was an upsurge of church building, not least in the Portadown area.

In the Church of Ireland, St Mark’s Church was enlarged in 1861. Lurgan Parish Church had its number of communicants doubled, and its present building, the largest parish church in Ireland, can be said to be a result of the Revival. Hill Street, Lurgan and Belleville Presbyterian Churches could also be regarded as products of the Revival.

The Methodists of Portadown decided in 1859 that their church was too small, and the present Thomas Street church was erected in 1860. In the 1860’s, Methodists built new churches at Edenderry and Derryall, and a preaching station at Edgarstown; while the historic church at Derryanville had to be enlarged to cope with increased attendances.

In the years 1860-70, 43 new Presbyterian congregations were formed in Ireland, although the population of the country as a whole was declining.

It is against this background that the discussions on opening a new church must be seen. At a meeting of Armagh Presbytery in June 1865, Rev Jackson Smyth referred to the growing population of Portadown, and asked for a Commission of Presbytery to confer with Rev L. D. Elliott (of First Portadown) and his officers on the state of the Presbyterian cause in the town. Meetings were held over the next two years to discuss the matter, and the first solution tried was the obtaining of assistance for Mr Elliott. Then the Church Extension Committee of the General Assembly sent a licentiate to work among non-churchgoers, and to attempt to form them into a congregation.

For the reasons we have suggested, thoughts at this time turned easily to the idea of founding new churches; and in these years after 1865 it gradually became evident that a number of Presbyterians in the town believed that the best way to cater for the needs of the district was to form a new congregation at the other end of the town. In 1867 a petition was sent to the Armagh Presbytery, and from there to the Synod Meeting in First Portadown in May 1867. (For convenience, I refer to the older congregation at Edenderry as “First Portadown”, even though it was then referred to as “Portadown Presbyterian Church”. There could not be a First Portadown until there was a Second Portadown!). The Synod reported to the General Assembly next month, that it had received a Memorial from 105 persons residing in Portadown, requesting permission to establish a church and call a minister, and promising a Stipend of £30-6-6, of which £20-9-0 was to be provided by members of the group, and the remainder by friends.

On June 4th 1867, the General Assembly minutes record, “the Assembly agreed to form a second congregation in Portadown, to be under the care of the Presbytery of Armagh”.

Second Portadown had thus obtained its charter, but the real work remained to be done.

The situation was made more confused by the fact that while these negotiations were taking place, another group of Presbyterians had approached the United Presbyterian Church, a body based in Scotland, and had gone ahead with the formation of a United Presbyterian Church, which met at first in the Victoria Hall, David Street (now demolished). This group built a new church in West Street (later known as the Temperance Hall). That there was no animosity between the new churches is shown by the fact that when this new West Street church was opened, on July 18th 1868, the new minister of Armagh Road was present as a guest. The United Presbyterians did not prosper, and closed down in 1877. A Mr Cuthbertson was called as Minister, the church building was erected in West Street, and a few years later another minister, Mr Murray arrived.

But he ministered to declining congregations, and in 1877 he resigned and the Church closed. The building was eventually bought in 1899 by some Temperance Bodies, and re-named The Temperance Hall; it was later a Nursery School, and more recently has been used as shops.

In late 1867, the prospective members of the new Second Portadown congregation met in the Town Hall (a building situated at the junction of High Street and Woodhouse Street, where Burnett's shop used to stand, and which is now the Halifax Building Society). The first minister, Rev Samuel Andrews, was called, and ordained by the Armagh Presbytery on February 10th 1868. All was now ready for the official formation of the congregation.

Second Portadown Presbyterian Church was formed on February 23rd 1868, at a meeting in the Town Hall, when a Committee of 16 members was elected. It had as yet no Session, and no building; nevertheless we rightly celebrate this as the opening date, since the essentials were there – a lawfully constituted body met under an ordained minister for the worship of God and the administration of the Sacraments.

Ministry of Rev Samuel Andrews (1868-1886)

Armagh Road's first Minister was born in 1839 and licensed in the Ballymena Presbytery. His first church was Armagh Road, where he was ordained on February 10th 1868, and where he remained until his resignation on October 16th 1886. He then spent a year as Minister of Westport, Co Mayo, before emigrating to the U.S.A. in 1888. There he remained until he was killed in an accident at a railway crossing, at Fairbolt, Minnesota on March 29th 1901.

The Church Committee held its first business meeting on March 11th 1868. All members were present. Joseph Acheson was elected secretary and John Fulton treasurer. Three decisions were taken:

1. To erect a church building. A subscription list was opened with £220 contributed by the Minister and Committee.

2. To approach the Duke of Manchester (who owned the town) to obtain a site.

3. To order 25 copies of the Missionary Herald – the forerunner of the Presbyterian Herald. Those who were too poor to buy copies were to get them free.

On April 27th, the Minister was able to report that he had met the Duke of Manchester's agent, and that the Duke had offered a site for a church and manse, with a frontage of 80 feet, for an annual rent of £10, £5 of which would be paid back into church funds.

Armagh Road Church Before 1904

Building the Church

When the good news about the site was received, the work of erecting the building went ahead with great speed and enthusiasm. Plans were drawn up by Mr Boyd,

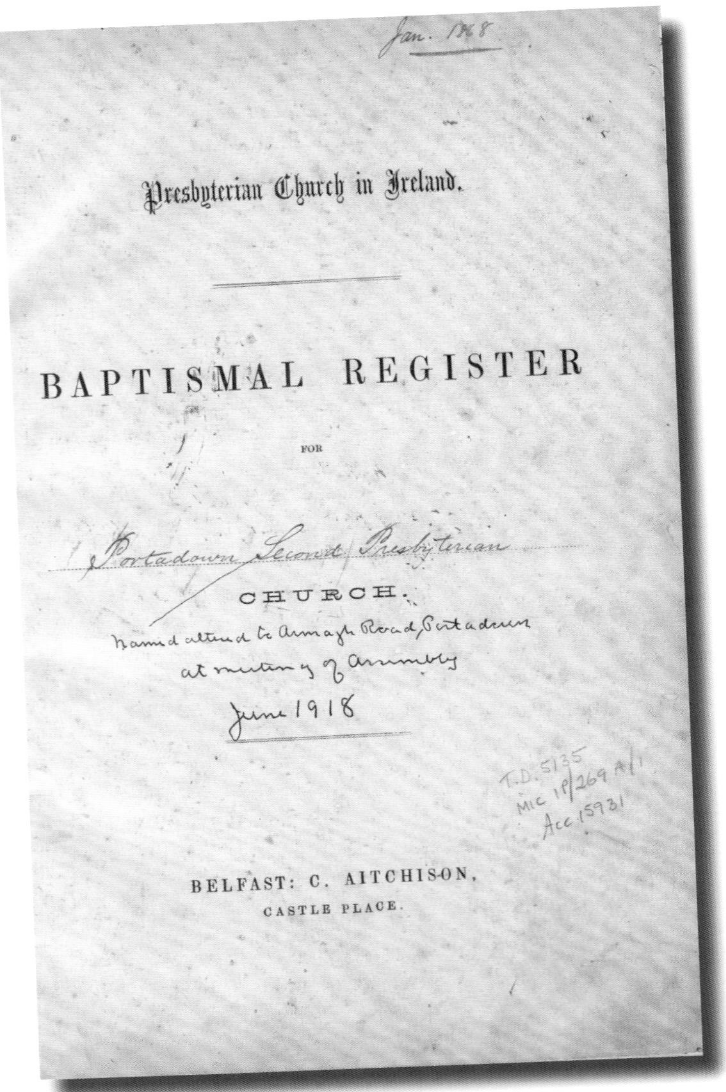

Jan. 1868

Presbyterian Church in Ireland.

BAPTISMAL REGISTER

FOR

Portadown Second Presbyterian

CHURCH.

Name altered to Armagh Road, Portadown at meeting of Assembly June 1918

T.D. 5135
MIC 1P/269 A/1
Acc 15931

BELFAST: C. AITCHISON,
CASTLE PLACE.

The official name of the Church was then Second Portadown Presbyterian Church, and so it remained until 1918, when the General Assembly agreed to the Church's request that the official name be changed to Armagh Road Presbyterian Church, which was already the commonly-used name

of the Belfast firm of Boyd and Batt, and a local contractor, Mr John Collen, was appointed. By October 1868, the building was well on its way; a first payment of £175 had been made to the contractor; and over £680 had been collected from various sources, including £250 from the General Assembly's Church and Manse fund. Four months later the Committee was settling the final details for the opening arrangements! Not only was the church completed by March 1869, but it had a gas lighting system installed, a five foot wall around the building, and all the interior furnishings. It seems almost unbelievable to us today that without any motor transport, power tools, electricity or telephones, the time needed, from the approval to build to the opening ceremony, was under 11 months.

The final accounts showed that the building had cost £838-13-6, plus £70-19-6 for architect's fees. Of this amount, £160 had to be borrowed; the remainder had been collected by the opening date. Despite these financial needs, the Committee decided in February 1869 that the surplus of the Sunday collections should be given to the poor of the congregation.

Opening the Church

The church on the Armagh Road was opened on Sunday, 21st March 1869 by Dr James Morgan, one of the leading churchmen of the time. His own church was at Fisherwick Place, Belfast, located where Church House now stands; the Fisherwick congregation moved to the present Fisherwick Church some years later. We are fortunate that Dr Morgan recorded his own impressions of the opening in his autobiography:

"May 27th 1868. On last Sabbath I was in Portadown, opening a new church there. Dr Porter was to have been with me, to preach one of the sermons, but he was unwell, and his duty, therefore, fell upon me. Thus I had two lengthened services – one at twelve o'clock, and the other at seven. The day was beautifully fine, and the congregation filled

the church twice. I preached with great ease and comfort, nor did I afterwards feel fatigue. I stopped with my friend and kinsman, Dr Massaroon, the Wesleyan minister, and was most comfortably and hospitably entertained. What an old age God gives to him and his wife, who is sister to Mrs Morgan. They were lovely in their youth, these two sisters, and God has given them both a lovely old age ...

The *Belfast Newsletter* described the opening ceremony as follows:

"On Sunday last, the newly-erected Presbyterian Church – the second in Portadown – was formally opened for public worship by stated services, over which, at noon and in the evening, the Rev Dr Morgan presided.

This site chosen for the new building is but a short distance from the town, on the Armagh Road, in the centre of a largely extended building district, the property of the Duke of Manchester, which will, ere long, be principally devoted to private dwelling-houses, a large number having already been erected and occupied. The style is Gothic, from the designs of Messrs Boyd and Batt, Belfast, and the execution, entrusted to Mr John Collen, has been carried out with a skill and promptitude which have earned for the industrious contractor many hearty encomiums.

The imposing frontage is built of limestone, with freestone dressings, and ornamented by a large central window, filled in with cathedral glass and stained glass margins, having moulded jambs, arch and bosses elegantly carved, likewise in freestone from the Dungannon quarries of Mr Kennedy, the neatly pointed gable being surmounted by a pinnacle with carved finial. Over the two doorways, in the recesses on either side of the main frontage, two neatly-formed quarter foot-lights are placed, with stone dressings, hood mouldings and carved bosses. Accommodation has been provided for 350 of a congregation, and the pews are of pine, varnished, this portion of the work having been entrusted to, and satisfactorily performed by Mr Joseph Wright, Jun.

2nd Presbyterian Church, Portadown - Carleton House view

The attendance at morning and evening services was numerous and influential, and must have proved exceedingly encouraging to the promoters of the newly-formed congregation. The venerable preacher selected as his text the 22nd verse of the 20th chapter of the Gospel of John; in the evening the 13th Verse of the 14th chapter of Revelation, from which he delivered filling and eloquent discourses. Messrs T. A. Shillington, J. P., John Hancock, J. P., Thomas Carleton, Averell Shillington, Robert Kernan and John McCammon acted as collectors in the morning; and Messrs W. J. Paul, Adam C. Capper, George Kinkead and Robert Glass officiated in a like manner at the evening service. Collections, including subscriptions, amounted to upwards of forty pounds".

It should be said that most of the distinguished townsmen who acted as collectors were not members of the congregation; they were invited guest collectors, according to the custom of the time.

A week after the opening, the Committee had a pleasant duty to perform – making a presentation to the keeper of the Town Hall for his services while the congregation worshipped there. They were now in their own building, whose appearance has not changed greatly since then. From the road, especially, the only major change is that there were originally two doors in the recesses now occupied by windows, and no central door. The church was shorter, and there was no organ, a precentor being employed to "conduct the psalmody". There was as yet no Manse or Church Hall.

Mr Andrews had the difficult task of organising a new congregation, clearing the debt on the church and having the school erected. In all of this he seems to have been an energetic and successful leader, raising much of the money himself by going on preaching and lecturing tours in England and Scotland.

In addition, he had considerable literary ability. If you turn over the pages of church magazines of the time – The Monthly Messenger, The Evangelical Witness, The Presbyterian Churchman, etc. – you will frequently find articles and poems by Samuel Andrews. His subjects were very varied – a series of articles on Scripture Characters, a poem on Queen Victoria's Jubilee, all flowed from his pen. A little book entitled "Irish Nationalism" was published for him in Portadown in 1884.

But his main subject was English Literature. He lectured and wrote extensively on this, and his major work was a lengthy book entitled "OUR GREAT WRITERS: Being Familiar Chapters on Some Leading Authors", published by Elliot Stack in London in 1884. One journal, looking forward to its publication, said, "We have no doubt it will be characterized by Mr Andrews' well-known dash and vigour of thought and style". The book had chapters on many of the leading English writers, beginning with Chaucer and ending with a chapter

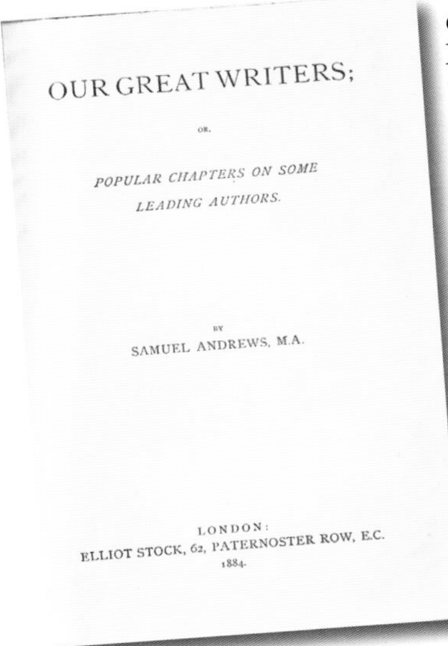

OUR GREAT WRITERS;

OR,

POPULAR CHAPTERS ON SOME LEADING AUTHORS.

BY

SAMUEL ANDREWS, M.A.

LONDON:
ELLIOT STOCK, 62, PATERNOSTER ROW, E.C.
1884.

on Tennyson's "In Memoriam"; (Tennyson would have been a modern writer at that time).

Mr Andrews' lectures on literature seem to have been particularly popular in Newry, where 40 guineas were collected as a gift for him when he left Portadown.

When the church opened in 1868, there were just sixty families claiming membership. In four years this number had risen to over 80, and there the number remained until the 1890's. The number of communicants on the roll was around 60 to 70. The number of Sunday School pupils on roll varied widely, from 45 to 125; and the total annual income of the church in its early years rose gradually from £80 to £162 in 1880.

That the church had to struggle to survive is shown by the fact that in 1871 the church had to dispense with the services of a precentor to save funds, Mr J. Fulton undertaking to lead the singing. Because of such measures, the debt was reduced by a little each year.

2nd Presbyterian Church, Portadown - From Photo by A. E. Jones, Portadown

The first Visitation of Presbytery took place in 1869. The congregation was congratulated on "the erection of this substantial and tasteful house of worship", and the Presbytery made three recommendations – that Ruling Elders be chosen as soon as possible, that a Congregational Library be started, and that the building be insured.

Mr Andrews had his own problems at times. On 8th July, 1877, he preached a sermon which caused some controversy in the town. Mr Andrews felt he was misunderstood, and decided to publish the sermon as a booklet, at his own expense, under the title "On Party Spirit". Some sentences read:

PREFACE.

THE multitude of different texts to be found in the acts and thoughts of our Literary Men is so great, that the commentary never needs to be a repetition of what was formerly written. And were it otherwise, this little book seeks to occupy a vacant place, by acting as an interpreter between higher authors and the ordinary reader, who is sometimes repelled by the dryness of literary history, as found in compendiums, and even in essays written in a learned or technical style. The aim of the Author of this Work has been, by avoiding unnecessary detail, difficult language, or involved phraseology, to interest English readers in the lives and thoughts of some of our greatest Writers, who are indeed familiar names, but often nothing more. Those who have not received a collegiate education sometimes take it for granted that the great classics of our tongue are too high and difficult for them. This book aims at making such persons feel that those Great Writers might all have one motto describing themselves and their works—'I am a man, and everything human interests me.'

It is also hoped that the Book will demonstrate that the

BURNS. 187

seven—what might he not have accomplished had he lived till three-score? Calumnies, according to their own base nature, seem peculiarly ready to cluster round genius—they have even polluted his grave, as if it were that of a drunkard slain by his dissipation. This was what some saw in the sad event, in which deeper eyes beheld a gift too soon recalled from a nation that learned too late to prize it. I will not admit that his faults were such as to excuse the neglect of his countrymen; for his faults he has himself pleaded such excuse as the candid and generous will not reject:

'Who knows the heart, 'tis He alone
Decidedly can try us,
He knows each chord, its various tone,
Each spring—its various bias;
Then at the balance let's be mute,
We never can adjust it;
What's done we partly may compute,
But know not what's resisted.'

Foreword by the author Samuel Andrews

BAPTISMAL REGISTER FOR 2d Portadown CHURCH.

NAME OF THE CHILD.	NAME OF FATHER.	NAME OF MOTHER.	DATE OF BIRTH.	DATE OF BAPTISM.	BY WHOM BAPTIZED.
Elizabeth Carson	William Carson	Jane Carson	11 March 1867	20 Feb. 1868	Rev. Samuel Andrews
James Edwards	James Edwards	Jane Edwards	16 July 1867	20 Feb. 1868	Rev. Samuel Andrews
Richard Fitsimmons	Benjamin Fitsimons	Alice Fitsimons	12th September 1861	20 Feb. 1868	Rev. Samuel Andrews
Amelia Conley	James Conley	Margt A. Conley	2d February 1868	23 April 1869	do.
Susan Finlay	Martha Finlay	William Finlay	2d November 1867	23 April 1868	do.
William John McBride	William McBride	Mary Jane McBride	15 April 1868	26 May 1868	do.
Anne Glassey	James Glassey	Jane Glassey	19 September 1867	9th July 1868	do.
John Proctor	George Proctor	Margaret Proctor	8th 1868	2d Decr 1868	do
Sarah Jane Proctor	"	"	14th Feb. 1866	2d Decr 1868	do.
William John Irwin	William John Irwin	Mary Carr	23rd July 1868	16th Decr 1868	do.
George Thomas Bingham	Thomas Bingham	Eliza Bingham	15 Augt 1868	13 Decr 1868	do.
William George Taylor	George Taylor	Sarah Taylor	26 Oct. 1868	30th Jan. 1869	Rev. Samuel Andrews
Anne Jane Wilkinson	Samuel Wilkinson	Jane Wilkinson	12 January 1869	22 March, 1869.	Rev. Samuel Andrews
Euphemia Petrie	William Petrie	Mary Anne Petrie	8 December 1868	4 April 1869	Rev. Samuel Andrews
Jane McBride	William McBride	Aramelia McBride	2d January 1869	4 April 1869	Rev. Samuel Andrews
Samuel Ennis	William Ennis	Eliza Ennis	3 January 1869	12 April 1869	Rev. Samuel Andrews
Martha Jane Finlay	William Finlay	Martha Finlay	12 Decr 1868	21 April 1869	Rev. Samuel Andrews
William Henry Joyce	Henry Joyce	Hannah Joyce	12 March 1869	28 April 1869	Rev. Samuel Andrews
Thomas Edward Conley	James Conley	Margt Ann Conley	6 April 1865	2 August 1865	Rev. Saml Andrews
William James Conley	James Conley	Margt Ann Conley	7 March 1871	4 April 1871	Rev. S. Andrews
James Brown	James Brown	Jane Brown	22 Sep 1869	3 Jan. 1869	Rev. Saml Andrews
William Archer	George Archer	Mary Archer	10 Decr 1868	8th Feb. 1870	Rev Saml Andrews
William John Carson	William Carson	Elizabeth Carson	16th March 1870	15 Sept 1870	Rev. Saml Andrews
James Thomson	Robert J. Thomson	Mary Thomson	7th July 1868	25th Sept 1870	Rev. S. Andrews
Rebecca Taylor	George Taylor	Sarah Taylor	5th Sept 1870	24th Jan 1871	Rev Saml Andrews.
Samuel James Bingham	Thomas Bingham	Eliza Bingham	11th Oct. 1870	9th April 1871	Rev S. Andrews
Anne Archer	George Archer	Mary Archer	18th June 1870	7 Oct. 1870	Rev. S. Andrews
Samuel Joyce	Henry Joyce	Hannah Joyce	15th Nov. 1870	16th Nov 1870	Rev. S. Andrews
William Brown	James Brown	Jane Brown	12th June 1871	14th Sept 1871	Rev. S. Andrews.
Robert John Dixon	William Dixon	Jane Dixon	3d Oct 1871	14th Oct 1871	Rev. S. Andrews

First Baptism in Second Portadown – Armagh Road Presbyterian: Elizabeth Carson, daughter of William and Jane Carson, born 11th March 1867 and baptised 20th February 1868 by Rev Samuel Andrews

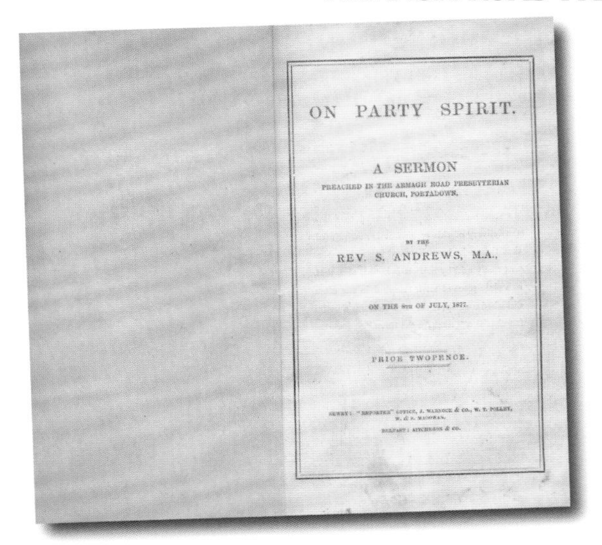

ON PARTY SPIRIT.

A SERMON
PREACHED IN THE ARMAGH ROAD PRESBYTERIAN CHURCH, PORTADOWN.

BY THE
REV. S. ANDREWS, M.A.,

ON THE 8th OF JULY, 1877.

PRICE TWOPENCE.

NEWRY: "REPORTER" OFFICE, J. WARNOCK & CO., W. T. POLLEY, W. & S. MACOWAN.
BELFAST: AITCHESON & CO.

"Those who are foremost in the Protestant cause should be the most eminent Christians in the community - they should be noble-minded, and pure-minded, and generous, and holy, and self-sacrificing, like Christ...Thus have I delivered my feeble testimony in favour of what I understand to be true Christianity. In this strain I have spoken among you these ten years — as a public preacher standing alone in this town — heard even by some of my own people with unwilling ears. However, I claim the right of satisfying my own conscience in this matter...I never meddle with politics. My business is simply to make the Christianity of the New Testament clearly understood."

The elders were not appointed until 1874, the church apparently managing quite well for its first six years without any!

In March 1874, three elders were ordained – John Chisholm Fulton, John Forbes and Joseph Acheson – and the first meeting of Session was held on April 3rd 1874.

Minutes of the Session
of the
Second Presbyterian Church, Portadown.

beginning
March 11th 1874

Portadown;
11th March; 1874.

We whose names are hereunto subscribed believe the Westminster Confession of Faith as described in the Book of the Constitution and Discipline of the Presbyterian Church in Ireland (Chap. II. sec. 3) to be founded on and agreeable to the word of God, and as such we acknowledge it as the Confession of our faith.

(Signed) John Chisholm Fulton
Joseph Acheson
John Forbes

Pages from the First Minute Book

Portadown, August 3rd 1874

The Session met this Evng. in the Session Room at 8 o'clock for conference on the visitation of the congregation. The meeting was constituted by prayer by Rev. S. Andrews; after which Each member of Session gave an account of individuals & families whom he had visited and of the difficulties in the way of their attending public worship. It was found that by the visits of the Elders some who had been neglecting public worship had been induced to attend. The unanimous opinion of the session was that there should be in the congregation an annual collection for the poor.

(Signed) S. Andrews, Moderator.
John Forbes Clerk.

Portadown Friday evening Octr 2nd 1874
The full Session of the Church met at half past seven o'clock this evening, by appointment, to hear the examination of young persons desiring to become Communicants on the following Sabbath for the first time. Revd S. Andrews Moderator. After hearing the examination conducted by the Minister, the Session were unanimous in admitting Wm Callan to the Lords Table

(Signed)
Saml Andrews, Modr.
John Forbes Clerk

The Old Manse

WHIG, WEDNESDAY, MAY 6, 1891.

ARMAGH PRESBYTERY.—The Presbytery of Armagh met in Portadown yesterday for the visitation of the Armagh Road Church (Rev. R. Jeffrey's), at eleven o'clock a.m. The Rev. J. H. Hanna (moderator) presided. There were also present the Revs. John Elliott, W. J. Brown, Wm. Clements, James Forsythe (clerk), R. Jeffrey, W. J. Macaulay, R. J. Whan, R. J. Porter, A. M'Afee, and Mr. W. M. Clow, elder. Mr. J. C. Fulton, J.P., represented the Session, and Mr. Hugh Hegan and Mr. W. G. Fulton the Congregational Committee. After carefully inquiring into the spiritual and temporal affairs of the congregation, the Presbytery unanimously came to the following finding:—"The Presbytery are very much pleased with the answers received from Mr. Jeffrey and the representatives of the Session and Committee. The attendance at public worship they regard as exceedingly satisfactory. They are happy to find that, owing to the faithful and efficient pastorate of their brother the Rev. R. Jeffrey, the contributions to stipend, missions, and sustentation have been so largely increased; that so many members of the congregation contribute so liberally to the Sustentation Fund, and that the recommendation of the former visitation with reference to the payment of the interest on the loan from the Board of Works by the congregation has been carried into effect. They are also pleased to find that a second national school has lately been organised in connection with the congregation in the schoolroom adjoining the manse, and that it is being wrought with great efficiency and success. They note with pleasure the improvements which have been made in the church, and the neat and tasteful way in which the entire church property is kept. They recommend that an addition be immediately made to the Session, and that efforts be made to induce non-contributors to subscribe to the Sustentation Fund." Mr. Clements was appointed to exchange pulpits with Mr. Jeffrey on an early Sabbath, read the finding, and address the congregation thereon. The Rev. R. J. Porter, of First Keady, brought to the notice of the Presbytery the fact that Thomas Small, Esq., J.P., had most generously presented the congregation of First Keady with a beautiful residence known as "The Hermitage," with twenty acres of land attached, as a manse. The Presbytery heard the statement with great satisfaction, and passed a hearty vote of thanks to Mr. Small for his princely gift. The Presbytery were entertained at dinner by the congregation in the Imperial Hotel.

John Forbes was elected the first Clerk of Session, and the congregation was divided into three districts which the elders visited. The result of this was the realization that poverty was preventing many people from attending church, and it was decided to have an annual collection for the poor, who seem to have been often in the minds of Armagh Road members in these years. We have seen that the surplus of weekly collections was given to the poor; and there were already two boxes in the church to receive contributions for this cause.

The Manse was completed in 1874, and it was at this time that Mr Andrews toured England and Scotland to help raise money. He brought back £43, and the Committee was soon encouraged to think about building a school, and to begin negotiating for the additional space needed for the building and playground.

Another 30 feet of frontage was obtained from the Duke of Manchester, space at the rear was obtained from the Fair Green Committee, plans were drawn up by the same Mr Boyd, Mr Andrews went on his travels again to raise money (£10 from

The Academy School from 1879

Belfast, £7 from Newry) and a contract was agreed, the cost being £350. By 1879 the buildings were completed.

The upper floor was as yet unfinished; the church had to borrow £100 to buy desks and equipment; but a successful Bazaar in the Town Hall in 1879 raised £300. As a result the boundary wall and playground could be completed, and the Manse redecorated. Joseph Acheson, J. P., repainted the church at his own expense, and by the end of 1880 the congregation could feel proud of their efforts over 13 years in the life of the church.

The records show a certain amount of the pattern of church life at this time. Communion Services were held twice a year, in April and September, always preceded by a pre-communion service on Wednesday evening at which there was often a visiting preacher. There was the weekly prayer meeting, and an annual soiree. The Session recorded that they had cause for thankfulness at the attendance at the morning service; but as early as 1875 they were discussing ways of improving attendance at the evening service (obviously not just a twentieth-century problem).

Relations with other Churches seem to have been friendly. In 1875 a request from the United Services Committee for the use of the church was granted “on account of the Evangelical Alliance requesting Christians to unite in prayer during the first week of the year”. A regular and welcome visitor at this period was the Rev James Glasgow, D. D., who had been one of the Irish Presbyterian Church’s first two foreign missionaries, and who had retired to live with his daughter in Portadown (in the house which is now the home of Mr and Mrs Alan Whitten). He was a member of First Portadown, but sometimes joined Session meetings at Armagh Road, and often spoke at pre-communion and other services.

When John Forbes left the district in 1879, Mr John C. Fulton was elected Clerk of Session, a post he held for the next 39 years. His father acted as Treasurer for the first 20 years of the church’s existence (1868-88).

Friday Evg. 1st May 1891

Rev R J Shaw preached in the Church this Evg. previous to the Communion to be celebrated on Sabbath 3rd May 1891. after which Rev R Jeffrey constituted the Session by prayer. Tokens were distributed. Miss Kate Nesbitt was admitted by certificate.

R. Jeffrey Mod.

John C. Fulton, Sess Clk.

Portadown 6th Nov. 1891

"We do hereby declare that we believe the Westminster Confession of Faith, as described in the book of the Constitution and Government of the Presbyterian Church in Ireland (Chap II Par 20) to be founded on and agreeable to the Word of God, and as such we subscribe it as the Confession of our faith"

William Ennis
William G. Fulton
Hugh W McCammon

Signed at a meeting of the Presbytery of Armagh held in the 2nd Portadown Presb. Ch. 6th Nov. 1891 for the Ordination of Elders.

Robert James Shaw, Mod. Presb.
James Forsythe, clerk.

The new elders of 2nd Portadown, signed the Westminster Confession at their ordination on 6th November 1891

Ministry of Rev Robert Jeffrey, M. A. (1887-1895)

After the resignation of Rev Samuel Andrews, Armagh Road Church called as its second Minister the Reverend Robert Jeffrey. Mr Jeffrey was born in 1839 in Greyabbey, Co. Down, where his father, Rev David Jeffrey, was the Presbyterian Minister. He was licensed by the Ards Presbytery in 1867, and after a period assisting an infirm Minister in Glenwherry, he was called to succeed his father at Greyabbey in 1873. From there he left for India, and spent the six years from 1878 to 1884 there, as Minister with the Free Church of Scotland Congregation in Bombay. He then returned to Ireland, to Mallow, until February, 1887, when he was installed in Armagh Road Church. He remained in Armagh Road until his untimely death in 1895.

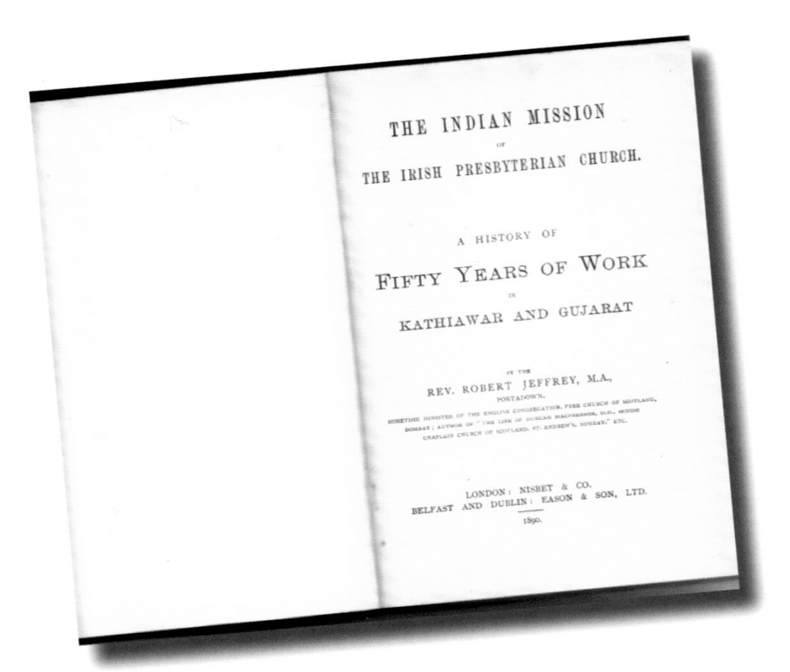
THE INDIAN MISSION
OF
THE IRISH PRESBYTERIAN CHURCH.

A HISTORY OF
FIFTY YEARS OF WORK
IN
KATHIAWAR AND GUJARAT

BY THE
REV. ROBERT JEFFREY, M.A.,
PORTADOWN,
SOMETIME MINISTER OF THE ENGLISH CONGREGATION, FREE CHURCH OF SCOTLAND, BOMBAY; AUTHOR OF "THE LIFE OF DUNCAN MACPHERSON, D.D., SENIOR CHAPLAIN CHURCH OF SCOTLAND, ST. ANDREW'S, BOMBAY," ETC.

LONDON: NISBET & CO.
BELFAST AND DUBLIN: EASON & SON, LTD.
1890.

Mr Jeffrey continued the literary tradition which Mr Andrews had begun. His most substantial work was his book, "The Indian Mission of the Irish Presbyterian Church", published in 1890 to mark the fiftieth anniversary of Irish Presbyterian Missions in India.

This book of 280 pages became the standard work on the subject. Articles by him appear frequently in journals of the time, and it is clear that Missionary Work was the subject which interested him most deeply, and which provided the theme for much of his writing. Rev Robert Jeffrey could remember his father's account of the First General Assembly in 1840 and the impassioned address by the Scottish preacher, Rev Murray McCheyne, which accompanied the dedication of the first two missionaries.

It seems appropriate that Mr Jeffrey should have come to Portadown, where the Irish Presbyterian Church's first two missionaries, Alexander Kerr and James Glasgow, had such close links. James Glasgow was living in retirement with his daughter

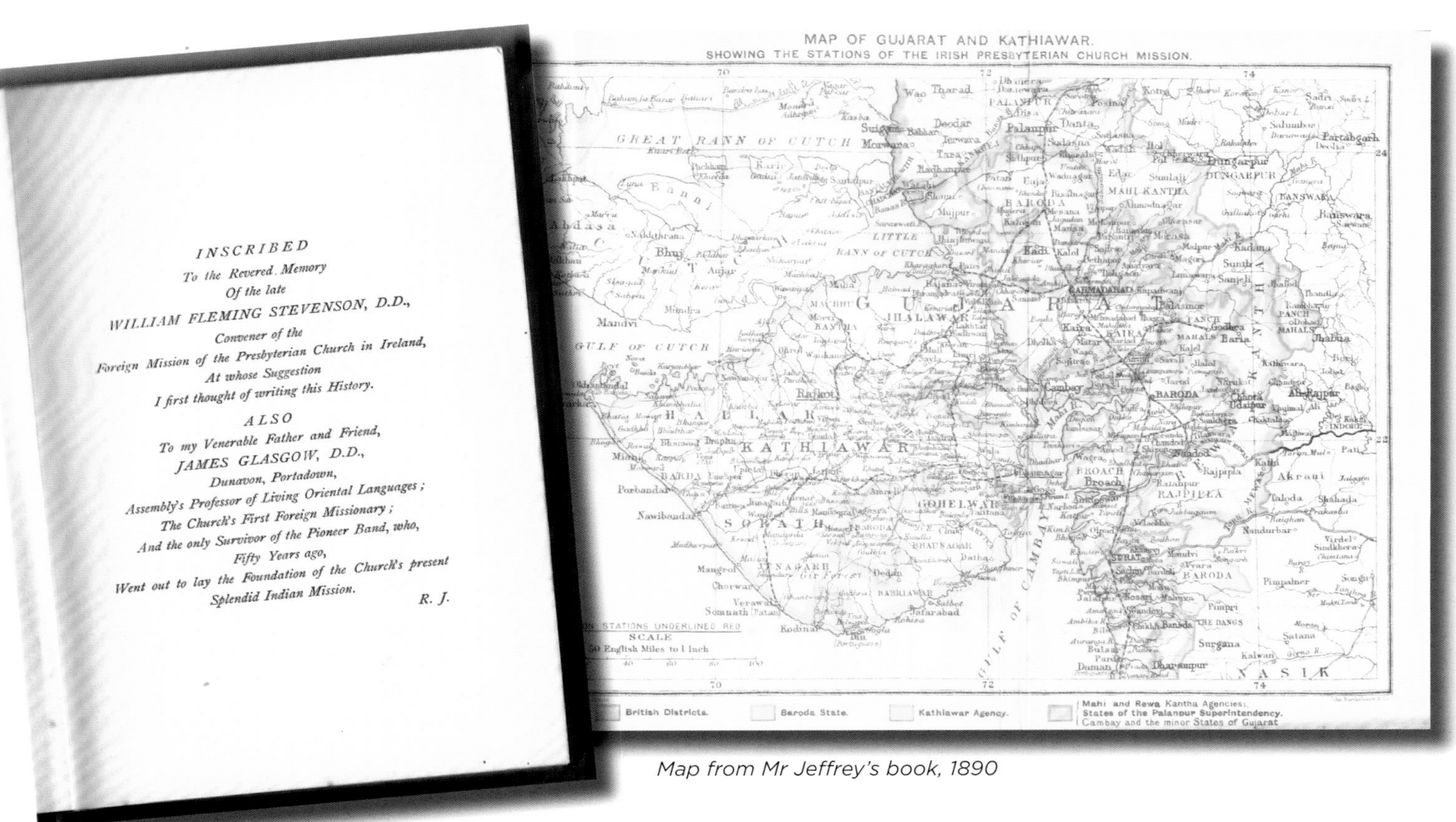

INSCRIBED
To the Revered Memory
Of the late
WILLIAM FLEMING STEVENSON, D.D.,
Convener of the
Foreign Mission of the Presbyterian Church in Ireland,
At whose Suggestion
I first thought of writing this History.

ALSO
To my Venerable Father and Friend,
JAMES GLASGOW, D.D.,
Dunavon, Portadown,
Assembly's Professor of Living Oriental Languages;
The Church's First Foreign Missionary;
And the only Survivor of the Pioneer Band, who,
Fifty Years ago,
Went out to lay the Foundation of the Church's present
Splendid Indian Mission.

R. J.

Map from Mr Jeffrey's book, 1890

in Portadown, and was able to help Mr Jeffrey with access to his diaries and other information on the Indian Mission; and Alexander Kerr had been Minister of what is now First Portadown.
Mr Jeffrey had plans to write the biography of Dr Glasgow, but he died before he could do so (and it still has not been done).

Mr Jeffrey was installed on February 8th, 1887, and afterwards a dinner was held in the Imperial Hotel. Improvements to the church property continued; Mr W. G. Fulton put in a stained glass window in 1887, and the following year a new boiler was installed, the system starting debt free. The money for such ventures was raised partly by normal congregational subscription, but supplemented by three sources which seemed to be traditional in these early years:

1) a bazaar run by the ladies;
2) a lecture by a visiting speaker, for which there was an admission charge;
3) a gift from the Fulton family.

The Church continued the practice of running lectures to raise funds. On 22nd February Mr Jeffrey gave a lecture in the Church entitled "India: its people: their habits: their religions." Tickets were sixpence or one shilling each, proceeds going to repairs of school premises, etc. The

'Portadown News' reported on the lecture with perhaps a little sarcasm:

"The trying climate of India does not seem to have impaired the health of the Rev Robert Jeffrey. On Wednesday night after speaking forcibly for an hour and forty minutes on this subject he pulled up quite fresh; his descriptions were as clear and vigorous as the Indian sky which he described so beautifully."

When the Presbytery held a Visitation in 1891, the congregation was commended for good attendance at services, and increased giving to stipend and to missions. Presbytery advised that new elders should be appointed, and later that year William Ennis, William G. Fulton and Hugh W. McCammon were ordained. One of the new Session's deliberations was on the question of whether Communion Services should be held quarterly; but no change was made in the old pattern of two Communion Services per year.

The congregation was growing steadily, and by the end of Mr Jeffrey's ministry 93 families claimed membership of Armagh Road. There were 78 communicants, 75 Sunday school pupils, and the church was free of debt.

This steady progress was interrupted with startling suddenness when on October 21st, 1895 the congregation learned of the most unexpected death of their minister. Still quite a young man, he had been active in the work of the church right up to this day, and the factual account of what followed, in the Session minutes, conveys the sense of shock, and of sympathy for Mr Jeffrey's wife and family. The church was draped in black until the end of the month, and the church took responsibility for the funeral arrangements and expenses.

The death of Armagh Road's second minister in 1895 was so sudden that tributes kept coming in for weeks afterwards. Some recalled his ability as a writer. The editor of The Witness reminded readers that Mr Jeffrey had financed his education for the Ministry by working as a journalist for papers in Belfast and Dublin. Indeed this editor went so far as to say "I might say of him, with no disrespect to his memory that he gave to the Church what was meant for journalism", and paid tribute to Mr Jeffrey's vigorous style. "He was a master of vigorous rhetoric and forcible expression, and few men in the Assembly or out of it could get the better of him in a verbal or literary combat ... He was one of the kindliest and most warm-hearted of men, the most genuine of friends, the most honest, candid and out-spoken of critics".

But it was Mr Jeffrey's interest in Missions that brought most comment. His work in India has already been mentioned, and his return from Bombay seems to have been caused by the effects the climate was having on the health of his wife and family.

While in Armagh Road he gave great encouragement to a young teacher who was preparing to go as a missionary to China. This man, John Omelvena, the Principal of a local school, was ordained for the China Mission in Armagh Road Church in September 1895. After the Ordination Mr Omelvena said: "To my friend, Mr Jeffrey, who took me up when raw and inexperienced, who saw virtues in me which were not visible to ordinary eyes, who backed me in all my efforts, and who has for many years been a helpful counsellor and loving father I owe a special debt of gratitude; to the church of which he is pastor, to the individual members of that church... I tender my sincere and heartfelt thanks, and assure them that while life is given me I shall ever recall with delight the pleasant and happy times spent among them in Portadown."

Mr Omelvena worked as a missionary in Manchuria from 1895 until 1929, when he retired to Belfast. His colleagues sometimes feared that he worked too hard. He used his educational experience to devise a plan for the education in western Manchuria, which was copied in other parts of China.

Mr Jeffrey's remarks at the same ordination service show the depth of his feelings: "As most of you know I lost a son some time ago whom I intended for the mission field, and Mr Omelvena in the past few years has taken the place of a son in my heart, and my heart and prayers will follow him to China as they would follow one of my own flesh and blood. I trust that God will enable Mr Omelvena to adorn His doctrine, and in all things to discharge his duty as conscientiously and devotedly in the future as he has done in the past." The son referred to had died three years earlier, and some said that Mr Jeffrey's health never recovered from the loss.

One of Mr Jeffrey's other services to the Presbyterian Church was reported as follows in the Portadown News:

"After the awful shipwreck of the passenger steamer on the coast of Spain, by which Mrs Beattie, wife of Rev William Beattie, Indian Missionary; Dr Mary McGeorge, Miss Nesbitt, and others belonging to the Presbyterian Church, lost their lives, Mr Jeffrey was entrusted by the Mission Board with the tender but trying duty of going to the scene of the catastrophe to endeavour to identify the dead, secure relics of them as far as possible, and to see that fitting sepulture was given to the bodies recovered from the sad sea waves. This loving duty Mr Jeffrey discharged in the most satisfactory and successful manner, after a fatiguing journey, many difficulties, and not a few perils. His narrative to the Board of Missions on his return home was listened to with rapt attention, and told with a pathos that melted every heart."

A local Methodist Minister, Rev Joseph Angliss, said: "His faith in God was real and gave him inspiration. He was humorous sometimes to an unusual degree ... but he abounded in sympathy and had a large heart". His friend Rev S. McComb said in Elmwood Church, Belfast: "Robert Jeffrey is dead, and in the lone country churchyard where he lies, a part of my life lies buried too ... Impatient as he was with cant and solemn drivel, within his heart there ever burned the fire of a beautiful piety."

Mr Jeffrey was buried in Greyabbey, where both he and his father had served as ministers. He left a widow, one son and two daughters. The last mention of him in the Minutes of Armagh Road was many years later, on February 7th, 1922, when the Minister was asked to write to send condolences to Mr James Jeffrey, Belfast, on the death of his mother, Mrs Robert Jeffrey, widow of Armagh Road's second Minister.

But the work to which Mr Jeffrey devoted his life had to go on.

Six candidates were selected from a preliminary list; 1,000 handbills were printed giving details of when each candidate would preach a trial sermon; and near the turn of the year, Armagh Road's third Minister, Rev H. W. Perry, was chosen.

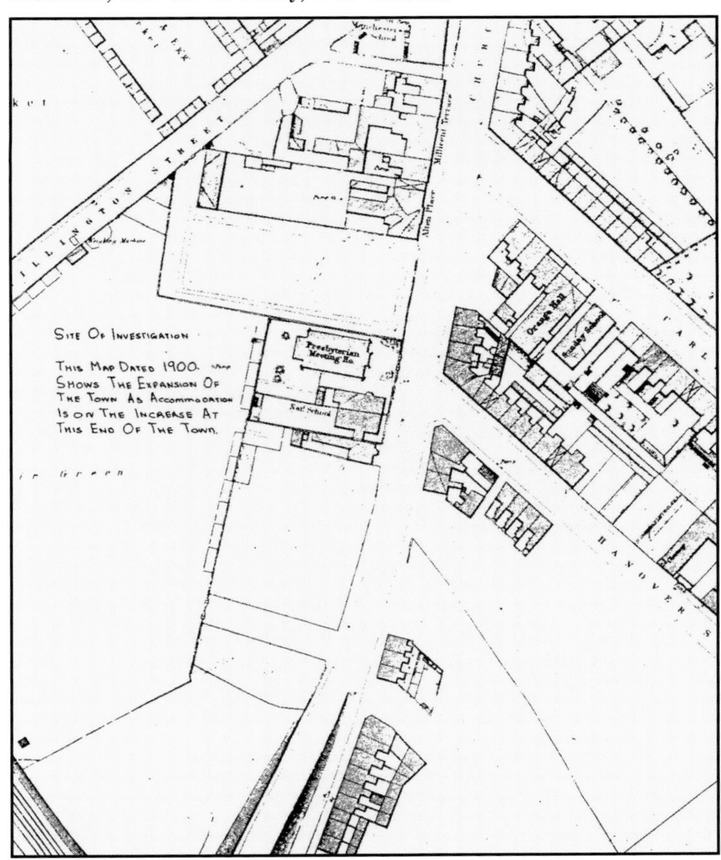

Town Map of 1900 shows increase of growing population

Ministry of Rev Hutchinson Wood Perry, B. A. (1896-1935)

REV. H. W. PERRY, B.A.
Minister 1896 - 1935

Mr Perry served in Armagh Road longer than any other Minister in the church's history, having completed almost forty years there when he retired.

He was born in Saintfield in 1865. After a ministry of seven years in Second Rathfriland Presbyterian Church (1889-1896), he was installed in Armagh Road on February 20th 1896; from this post he resigned on December 30th 1935. Later he became Resident Supply of Eglish Presbyterian Church, Dungannon, in 1936. He conducted services there until the Sunday before his death, which took place on January 7th 1942.

Among the events which followed the arrival of the new Minister, we note an invitation to Rev Mr Cregan, in July 1896, to lecture, with a view to introducing a kindergarden into the school. At the same time, Rev Charles Davey, a notable preacher of the time, was invited to conduct a series of special services. He agreed to come in November, and successful services were, in fact, held.

In 1897, the Session decided to have four Communion Services in the year, two in the morning and two in the evening. Minutes at this period are often concerned with mundane but necessary items such as repairs to the boiler, coats of paint, and changes of pew (for pews were still being let). Providing funds for the Sunday school was a recurring problem, often met by bringing along a visiting lecturer and taking up a collection. In these pre-radio days the appetite for lectures seems to have been insatiable.

As the twentieth century dawned, so did instrumental music. It began with a request to use an American organ at the Wednesday prayer meeting and praise service. The Session agreed, "provided none of those attending the prayer meeting have conscientious objections". Apparently none had.

The Session which agreed to this was now reduced to three members. This same year they divided the town into districts for supervision, Mr W. G. Fulton taking Edenderry, Mr J. C. Fulton Edgarstown and Mr W. McCammon Church Street.

Further discussion of the organ was deferred, because now a bigger project was beginning to be discussed in Armagh Road – the enlargement, or possible rebuilding, of the church.

The Enlargement of the Church, 1904

No basic structural changes had been made in the church since it was built. Repairs were now needed, but some members felt that the growth of the congregation, and the growth of the town, required a larger building.

The congregation had grown rapidly since Mr Perry's arrival, and it reached 140 families in 1905 – over twice its size when the church was opened. Portadown's population had grown also – from over 6,000 when the church was opened to over 10.000 in 1901. Edenderry Presbyterian Church had been enlarged to its present size in 1891.

On May 12th 1902, the Committee decided unanimously that the church should be enlarged, and Mr Houston, the architect, was asked to suggest plans. Next month the Committee decided to visit Donacloney church in search of ideas, and discussions took place on whether the existing church should be enlarged, or replaced by a new one. Members of the congregation were to be asked how much they would give towards the erection of a new church.

The architect reported that a new church, to accommodate 500 people on the ground floor, would cost between £3,000 and £4,000 pounds. Opinion came to favour enlarging rather than replacement. But what form was the enlargement to take?

Two transepts were suggested, but this plan ran into difficulties, as it was not possible to encroach upon Miss Carleton's wall or garden. The architect suggested a shallow transept at that side, and a deeper one at the opposite side, a plan which would cost approximately £1,300. This plan would, however, have given the church an unbalanced appearance, and fortunately it was dropped.

On April 21st 1903, the Committee instructed the architect to prepare a plan without transepts; the basic changes being to lengthen the church by 30 feet, and placing the main door in the centre. The congregation had already promised £700 for this work.

Arrangements were made for the congregation to occupy the Orange Hall for eight months while the work went on during the year 1904. The reopening was fixed for November 6th 1904, when Professor Hamill from Assembly's College, Rev Dr W. J. Lowe of Londonderry, and Rev Mr McMillan of Cooke Centenary Church, Belfast, took part in the services. The actual changes made are described in the next paragraph; it will be seen that the church has been changed very little since 1904.

The way past Armagh Road, early 20th Century, with a few late arrivals for church

Plans of the 1904 extension

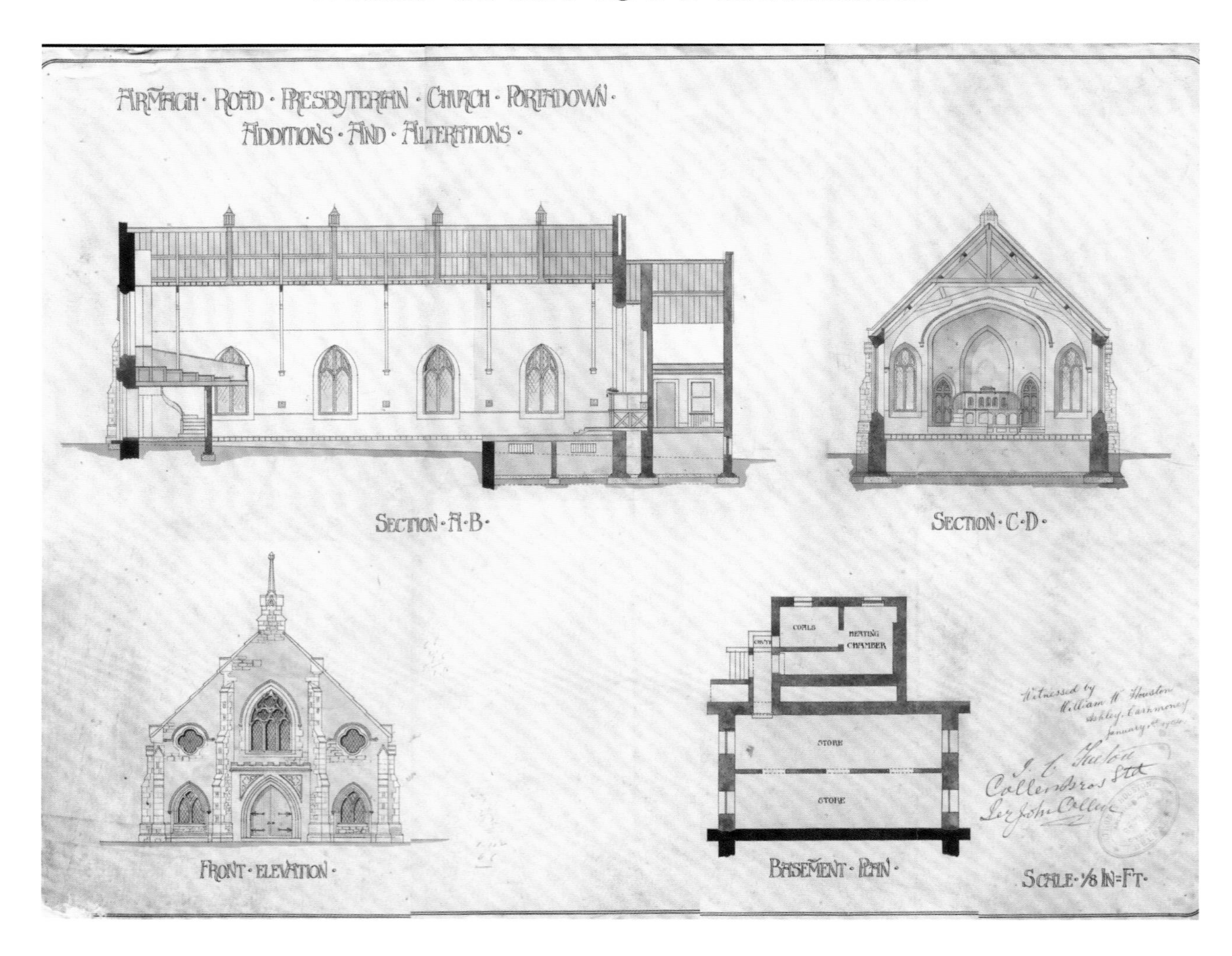

Plans of the 1904 extension. 22 feet were added to the church at the "pulpit end", and a new gallery built across the opposite end. In all, this provided an extra 172 seats, as well as more space for the choir, organ and communion table. The old Gothic front of the church was unchanged, except that a new central doorway was inserted; the two former side doors became windows.

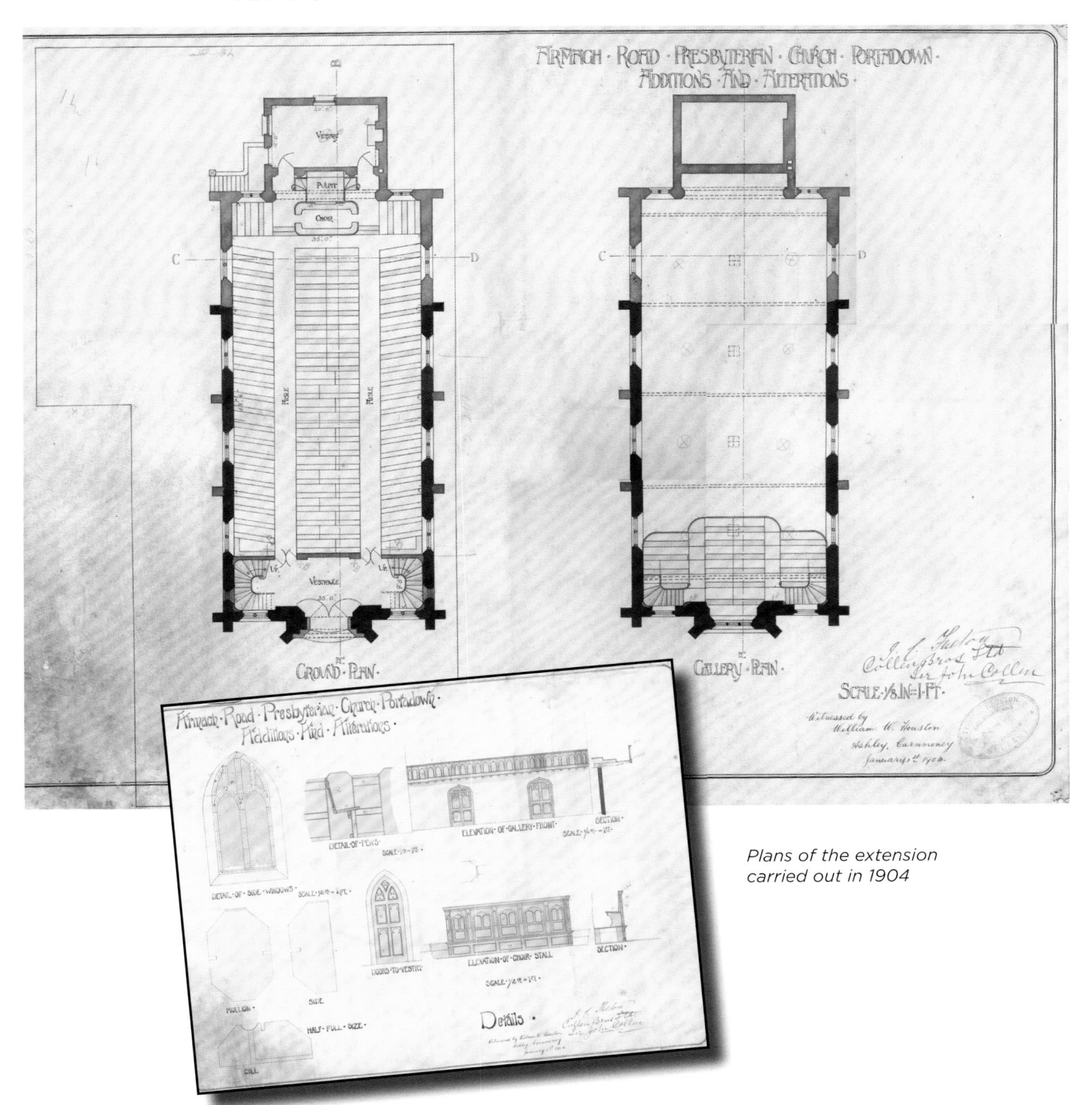

Plans of the extension carried out in 1904

Before 1904
Two doors and a bigger middle window

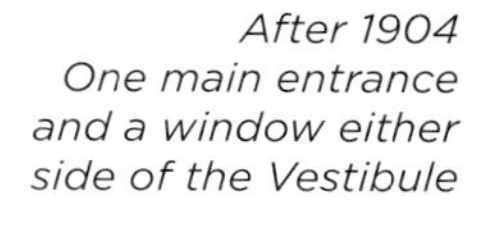

After 1904
One main entrance and a window either side of the Vestibule

One reason for changing to a central entrance doorway was that the new stairs leading to the new gallery would have partly blocked entry through the former two entrance doors. The new stairs also made the windows at each end of the vestibule useless, and you can still see where they have been blocked up. Windows were installed where these two entrance doors had been; the changes to the front of the church was added so skilfully that contemporary reports say that even then it was difficult to see, on the exterior of the building, where the new work began.

Inside, a new terrazzo floor and swing doors were added to the vestibule. The old plaster ceiling of the church was replaced by a diagonal sheeted ceiling, as at present, with pitch-pine mouldings and ornamental ventilators. Another change inside was the removal of the tie-rods, which had been inserted some years before when the walls were beginning to spread. (The buttresses outside took their place as supports for the side walls; they are still there.)

The old wooden-framed windows were replaced by the present ones, with concrete tracery and tinted glass.

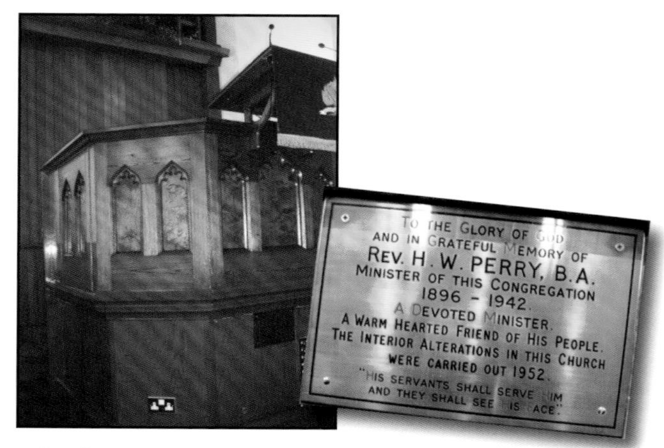

In the rear wall was put a deeply-recessed Tudor arch, and in this recess a pitch-pine pulpit with Gothic-style panels was placed.

New pews of pitch-pine were added, the old pews being grained to match. A low platform in front of the pulpit was provided for the choir. Also dating from this time are the two doors at either side of the pulpit, leading to the room at the rear, which was also reached from outside by a set of stone steps, and which had the heating chamber underneath. The inside walls were painted grey.

The architect for this work was Mr Thomas Houston, Kingscourt, Belfast. The final cost came to more than £1,900; a large sum, but it seems to have been well spent, since the church has not needed any large-scale alterations since.

Presbytery of Armagh.

Rev. W. CLEMENTS,
Clerk,
Benburb,
Co. Tyrone.

The Presbytery having heard the answers given by the Minister and the representatives of Session and Committee have pleasure in placing on record their entire satisfaction with the reports. They greatly rejoice in the emphatic testimony so freely borne to the fact that their esteemed Rev. W. Corry, B.A. continues to discharge all the duties of the pastorate with ability, earnestness and devotion, that he enjoys the confidence and respect of the people and that they are profiting by his labours among them; that the attendance upon the ordinances of God's house is so encouraging, especially at the Evening Service, and that the instruction of the young is so carefully attended to in the Sabbath and Day Schools. They are glad to learn that the members of Session cooperate so heartily with the Minister in the work and oversight of the Congregation; that the Congregational Committee to whom the finances have been entrusted are discharging their duties with wisdom and success, and that by the Divine blessing on the indefatigable labours of Minister and office-bearers there are abundant signs of healthy spiritual life and [illegible] in the Congregation.

The Presbytery very heartily congratulate the Congregation on the enlargement and beautifying of their Church at a cost of considerably over £1800, that this expenditure has been fully met and that they are free from debt. In this connection they cannot but express their satisfaction with the princely liberality of Mr [illegible] and Mr [illegible].

They regret that the number of those who profess the Lord Jesus Christ at His Table is not so large as might reasonably be expected, that family worship is not so generally observed as it ought to be, and they recommend the Session to direct the attention of all the families connected with them to these matters which are most vital to their spiritual life and prosperity.

It is a matter of gratification to the Presbytery that the contributions to the [illegible] have been steadily rising since their last Visitation, and without reflecting on those members who contribute so [illegible] they would affectionately urge all non-contributors to do their duty to this most important Fund for the maintenance of the Church in this land.

The Presbytery commend the Minister and Congregation to God and the word of His grace with the earnest prayer that He may continue to bless them in all things that pertain to their preparing for time and eternity, and appoint their Moderator Rev. J. Wilfrid Wright B.A. to read this finding and address the Congregation thereon.

Extracted from the records of the Presbytery of Armagh this 5th day of July, 1906 by me.

W. Clements Clerk

Letter of Presbytery from July 1906 congratulating the Congregation on the completion of the 1904 Church extension and the fact that all the bills were paid off very speedily

Architects' drawings for these extensions have in the past year been discovered and rescued by Mr Wilfred Moore, and are a valuable addition to our archives.

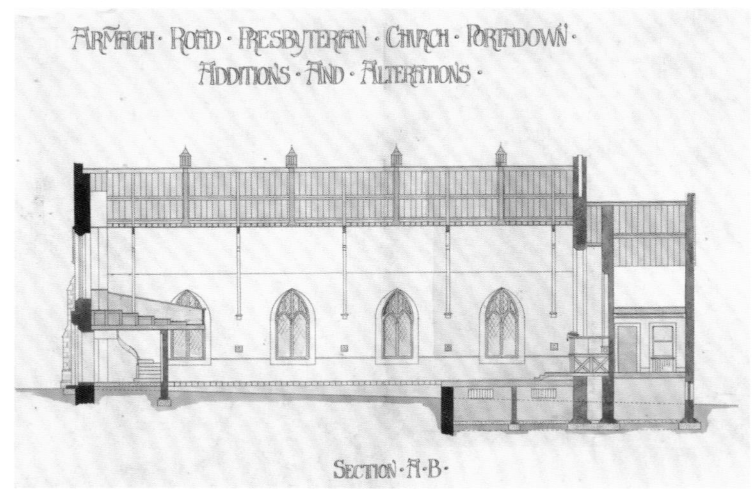

To see full plans see page 24 & 25

Remainder of Mr Perry's Ministry

While these extensions were being constructed, the question of instrumental music was again raised. This was a topic which was capable of arousing great excitement in the second half of the nineteenth century and in the early part of the twentieth, and in many churches there were long debates on whether there should be a church organ.

There were often similar controversies about whether the church should use hymns as well as psalms.

In Armagh Road, these questions seem to have been settled in a cool and matter-of-fact way. It was decided that an American organ should be used during the opening services in 1904, and that if it seemed satisfactory to the congregation, it should be retained. There is no record of any discord about its retention; and similarly when hymns were introduced in 1912 they seem to have been accepted readily.

THE PSALTER

A REVISED EDITION OF
THE SCOTTISH METRICAL VERSION
OF THE PSALMS WITH
ADDITIONAL PSALM-VERSIONS

Prepared and published by authority of the General Assembly of the Presbyterian Church in Ireland

LONDON
OXFORD UNIVERSITY PRESS
GLASGOW MELBOURNE

A1 Nonpareil

1912 Hymn Book

One piece of enterprise which deserves mention is the production of an operetta in 1908, which raised enough money to buy cooking equipment for the Academy school. In 1911 we again have record of a special sermon and collection to help the poor of the congregation.

September 28th 1912 was Covenant Sunday, and in Armagh Road, as in other Protestant Churches, special Covenant Day services were held to seek God's help in this critical time in Ulster's history.

In 1918 Mr J. C. Fulton died, and Mr W. G. Fulton died in 1925. These two events marked the end of an era. "We could not estimate rightly what he was to, and what he did for this congregation", recorded the Session and Committee on the death of J. C. Fulton. They referred to his exemplary attendance at services and prayer-meetings, and noted that he had been Clerk of Session for 39 years.
W. G. Fulton, at the time of his death, had been Treasurer for 37 years, and a Sunday school teacher for over 50 years. In addition, the Session referred to his regular attendance at services, prayer-meetings, choir and committee — never absent from any without sending his Minister an explanation.

Obituary for William Galway Fulton 1925

THE IRISH PRESBYTERIAN. Feb 1926

—o—

WILLIAM GALWAY FULTON

The subject of this brief sketch, who died at his residence, Alston, Balmoral, Belfast, on 2nd December, 1925, was born and lived all his life in Portadown. His father, John Fulton, as a young man came from the adjoining town of Lurgan, and established himself as a grocer. He was diligent in business, frugal in disposition, and in later years possessed a large wholesale and retail trade. He was twice married, his first wife being a Scotch lady named Chisholm, by whom he had one son and one daughter. The former, John Chisholm, joined his father in the business, in which he took an increasing interest as the years passed. Miss Fulton married a son of the late Rev. Dr. Houston, of Knockbracken. Mr. Fulton's second wife was a Miss Toye, sister to a Presbyterian minister in Belfast. By her he had one son, William Galway, and a daughter who died in early life. Ten years exactly separated the ages of the two brothers. The younger man also joined in the business, which continued for a short time after Mr. John Fulton's death, and was then wound up. It was my privilege to know

THE SECOND MRS. FULTON.

She was a lady of a type which, alas! is not so frequently met with nowadays. A woman of strong commonsense, a most devoted and devout Presbyterian, she loved her Church, and was willing to spend and be spent in its service. The only adornment she aspired to was the inward adornment of the mind and heart, which to her was of the utmost importance. She was one of those quiet, God-fearing women who sustain and encourage their minister by constant attendance at all the church's services. While diligent and successful in business, Mr. John Fulton proved himself a good citizen and supporter of the Church. He was a foundation member of the second congregation in Portadown, and contributed liberally, as did his sons, to the building fund.

Brought up in such surroundings it was natural to find the sons walking in their parents' footsteps. The subject of this sketch devoted himself to work in the Sabbath school, and in the report of the Sabbath School Society recently issued, his name appears in the list of teachers who received recognition during 1925, with a record of 53 years' service, which would show that he became a teacher when a lad in his teens. Released from an active business life ere he reached middle age, he threw himself energetically into works of philanthropy and mercy, and this in an ever expanding form, seldom allowing a new undertaking to displace an old one. Naturally the Church had a first claim, and as its treasurer he gave valued service. On every occasion on which it became necessary to raise special sums of money, he and his brother acted with great liberality. Indeed so much was this the case that after the death of the latter the congregation felt impelled to acknowledge its indebtedness by placing a tablet in the church vestibule.

MR. W. G. FULTON, PORTADOWN.

One cannot dwell in detail upon

THE NUMEROUS ACTIVITIES IN WHICH HE WAS ENGAGED.

The N.S.P.C.C. had in him a most active secretary and treasurer, and he was also treasurer of the U.S.P.C.A. Two temperance cafes in the town he helped to found, and acted as controller and accountant for many years. Prior to the establishment of a War Pensions office he acted as correspondent and adviser for numbers of poor women, and was so engrossed in this work that it became well-nigh impossible for him to take a holiday. While these things bulk largest in the public eye it is questionable if they are the most important. Who can calculate the real value of what Wordsworth describes as the best part of a good man's life—"his little nameless, unremembered acts of kindness and of love?"

"Where is your father," asked a stranger of a little girl who opened the hall door to his knock. "I really don't know" was the reply, "but I know he is away doing something for somebody." This in large measure describes the life we would portray. His own ambitions and wants were so few, he spent little time on them, while he squandered it freely on others. To him might be applied in a truer sense than to anyone else it has been the writer's experience to know, the words of Job—"When the ear heard me then it blessed me, and when the eye saw me it gave witness to me. Because I delivered the poor that cried and the fatherless and him that had none to help him. The blessing of him that was ready to perish came upon me, and I caused the widow's heart to sing for joy."

It was in quiet unobtrusive ways he occupied his time. He was quite willing to stand aside in favour of others in the more showy activities of life. Unlike his brother, he never aspired to a prominent part in the public life of the town, or even in the work of the Irish Presbyterian Church, in many of whose schemes he was much interested. For some years he acted as a Poor-Law Guardian, but this was the extent of his public services. He was much attracted by the work of the Salvation Army, to whose enterprises he was a liberal contributor, and he occasionally presided at their meetings. He enjoyed reading, as his well-stocked library, to which he kept constantly adding, bore evidence, as also did his powers of conversation; while gardening and walking were his favourite modes of recreation.

HIS OUTSTANDING CHARACTERISTICS

of this good man were unselfishness and humility. Nature and grace made him the man he was. He never had to fight hard battles against avarice and pride. One of the things he dreaded most was publicity. He was a living illustration of the wise man's thrice repeated proverb, "before honour is humility." When pressed by his friends to receive testimonials and addresses before leaving Portadown to reside in the city he refused, and they had to be prepared without his consent. At the presentation made to him by the congregation, he sat unmoved while others were visibly affected, and when asked afterwards why this was so he said—"Just because I could not realise that what they said of me was true."

Death came suddenly. Retiring at his usual hour he awoke from a restless sleep, complaining of difficulty in his breathing, and the end came before the hastily summoned doctor arrived. His memory will live in the hearts of large numbers of people who admired his character, as well as many who were sharers in his beneficence and his sympathy.

Mr. Fulton was happily married to Miss Alice Lang, daughter of a Moravian minister, who was likeminded with himself and a sharer in all his activities and good works. To her, and their son and daughter, the sympathy of a large circle has been expressed

W. M. C.

1st Portadown Guide Unit Armagh Road Presbyterian Church Circa 1920 - 30

Front Row: A. Black, G. Wilson, J. Radcliffe, R. Hull, H. Crozier, Susie Robbin Clayton

2nd Row: L. Black, L Radcliffe, L. Logan (Lieut), Miss Hagen (Capt), E. Radcliffe (Lieut), R. Greer, H. Tomes, J. Clayton

3rd Row: L. McClelland, P. Allen, A. Smart, M. Gordon, N. Newell, M. McCullough, I. Smart, M. Cooke, P. Clelland, I. Furgus

Back Row: M. Gibson, S. Bell, D. Black, M. Wright, F. Newell, H. Gordon, O. Hewitt

Since the opening of the church there had been a Fulton in at least one of the chief offices of the church. In particular, no one except a Fulton had ever been treasurer (until 1925) and the Presbytery in their Visitation after the 1904 extension took the unusual step of mentioning the Fulton family by name and recording gratitude for their generosity to the church.

Long service of this kind has not, however, been limited to one family, and we may record here such names as James G. Espie (Secretary 1895 - 1934), Joseph Nevin (Treasurer 1925 - 47, Secretary 1934 - 47, Clerk of Session 1947 - 53), Robert Mason (Clerk of Session 1924 - 47), Robert Cumming (Clerk of Session 1953 - 1989), and Rodney Spence (organist 1971 - to date).

In 1919 six new elders were appointed, the largest group to date — Hugh Hegan, Joseph Logan, Robert Mason, Andrew Barbour, George Hawthorne, and Thomas A. Hawthorne. A notable visitor this year was Rev Wylie Blue of Belfast, who conducted special services.

In this year also, a War Memorial was discussed. Various suggestions were made regarding the form it should take — a tablet, a manse, a hall, an organ. The decision was for a Memorial Tablet, which was unveiled in October 1921 by Major D. G. Shillington.

In 1921 the Weekly Freewill Offering scheme was introduced. The period between the two World Wars was difficult, financially, in many sectors of life, and there were times when the church had difficulty in making ends meet. Growth in the congregation seems to have been halted — the number of families was recorded as 140 in each of the years 1905, 1915 and 1930, and as less than that in some intervening years (135 in 1920).

Total church income varied greatly according to projects undertaken, but was often around £600 per annum.

In 1923 the two Presbyterian Churches in the town combined to sponsor a series of services by a notable evangelist of the day — "The Marèchale":

Mrs Evelyn Booth Clibborn, who was the daughter of William Booth, founder of the Salvation Army — and when the series was ended, both Sessions recorded their thanks to Mrs Clibborn and her daughter.

The number of communicants in these years averaged about 70, and this number remained fairly stable from 1919 until after 1945, when an increase began.

In 1924 the church sponsored a lecture in the Town Hall by Rev Joseph Hocking, a well-known writer of the day, entitled "The World in the Melting Pot". Tickets were sold at three shillings or one shilling, and total receipts were £36-7s, yielding the church a profit of £15.

Pew-rents were still in operation. The amounts had been fixed when the church was extended in 1904, and the annual cost of a "sitting" or single seat varied according to the position in the church: 3/- for seats to left and right of the pulpit, 4/- for the first four pews, 6/- for all seats from the fifth pew to the back of the church, 5/- for the front two rows of the gallery, and 4/- for other gallery seats.

Mr Don Stevenson - Principal of the Academy Primary School with one of the first school football teams. Back row: F. Wright, S. Donald, W. Brown, Principal Don Stevenson, M. McDonald, A. Watson, J. Russell. Front row: G. Crozier, T. Hall, Davie Cochrane (Later of Leeds United and N. Ireland) T. Totten and W. Hayes.

Financial difficulties in 1928 led to a cut in the Minister's salary, from £50 to £25 for the last quarter of the year. This was a time of unemployment and depression all over the world.

The drain on finances was somewhat reduced by the decision that year to transfer the Academy school to the Regional Committee of Education. Even so, at the end of the year, the Committee had to record: "It was agreed to ask Mr Perry to invite the ladies of the congregation to devise some means of relieving the debt on the congregation".

The struggle continued through the world-wide slump, and in 1930 and 1931 cuts had again to be made in the Minister's salary. An anonymous donation of £50 in 1931 helped the situation, and later gifts meant that despite these problems, the gas lighting system (this is how the church had been lit since it was built) was replaced by electricity in 1931.

As Mr Perry's ministry drew to a close in 1935, Armagh Road was a congregation of 130 families, free of debt. Mr Perry received many warm tributes on his retirement; and when he left early in 1936 to act as resident-supply at Eglish, the congregation presented him with an address which spoke, among other things, of his careful verse-by-verse expositions of the Scriptures at the mid-week services.

Mr Perry was popular also with his brother ministers. He had been Clerk of the Presbytery, and in 1939 a dinner was held in the C. B. Cafe, Armagh, to mark his Jubilee — fifty years in the Ministry. Professor Davey gave the assembled ministers a lecture on Jeremiah.

The Fulton Family

The most prominent memorial in Armagh Road Presbyterian Church is the plaque in the vestibule to the Fulton family. It reads:

THIS CONGREGATION WAS ORGANISED AND THE CHURCH BUILT IN 1868, THE LATE MR JOHN FULTON, PORTADOWN. TOOK A DEEP INTEREST IN THE ORGANISATION AND DEVELOPMENT OF THE CONGREGATION, AND WAS ONE OF THE LARGEST CONTRIBUTORS TOWARDS THE ERECTION OF THE CHURCH.

IT WAS ENLARGED AND RENOVATED IN 1904, LARGELY OWING TO THE GENEROSITY OF HIS SONS JOHN CHISHOLM FULTON, J.P. AND WILLIAM GALWAY FULTON, WHO HAVE ALWAYS TAKEN THE DEEPEST INTEREST IN THE CONGREGATION.

Memorial to the Fulton Family

Yet the Fultons are now remembered only in memorials and in some interest the church receives each year on their bequests. So, who were the Fultons?

John Fulton

John Fulton was one of the group who founded Armagh Road Presbyterian Church. He had been a member of the Committee of First Portadown Church, and seems to have come from Lurgan to establish a wholesale grocery business in Portadown. The business was at numbers 1 to 3 Market Street, but the fine family home was on the Armagh Road, very near to where the Church was built.

The Fulton home still stands; after the Fultons left the town it became known as the "Broo", the Employment Exchange; and it is where Mr Maurice Cushnie had his offices. The house was called Lismore House, (still its official name, Mr Cushnie tells me).

John Fulton was Treasurer of the new Church for its first 20 years, and steered the congregation through these difficult early years when a congregation of sixty families built the present building.

Before the church was built, there are references to meetings of the Building Committee being held in John Fulton's office. John Fulton's business had prospered, and he was personally generous to the church. Once in these early years when money was scarce, the congregation decided it could no longer afford to pay a precentor (that is, the person responsible for the music, and starting the singing in the days before an organ), and John Fulton volunteered to "raise the singing".

Yet John Fulton never became an elder. This must have been by his own choice, since he was the best-known member of the congregation, and was clearly well respected. When he died in 1888, he left a generous legacy to the church.

John Fulton was married twice, and each marriage produced a son who contributed much to the church. His first wife was a Scottish lady called Chisholm; they had a son, John Chisholm

Fulton, and a daughter who married a son of Rev Dr Houston of Knockbracken.

After the death of the first Mrs Fulton, John Fulton married a Miss Toye, who was the sister of Rev Tommy Toye, a famous Belfast minister. From this second marriage there came a daughter who died young, and another son, William Galway Fulton.

The Galway in the name seems to have come from the Toye family: Tommy Toye had married the daughter of a William Galway.

John Chisholm Fulton

The elder son, John Chisholm, joined his father in the business. He was ordained as one of the first three elders of Armagh Road, and was Clerk of Session from 1879 until his death in 1918.

He was Superintendent of the Sunday School for almost 50 years, resigning only a few weeks before his death. At his funeral service in Armagh Road Rev H. W. Perry said of Mr Fulton; "He died, as he wished to die, in harness. He loved the Courts of God's house, and his place in that church at the morning or evening services was never empty unless for some imperative reason. He gave very generously, and indeed sometimes in a princely fashion, to the funds of the church."

John Chisholm Fulton, known to his friends as "Chizzy", played a full part in the life of Portadown. He was Chairman of the Town Council, having been re-elected to that position a short time before his death, and the Council as a body attended his funeral.

He had been a Magistrate for 34 years, and at the next Court the Resident Magistrate summed up his colleague's service with the words "He tried to do right".

William Galway Fulton

The younger son, William Galway Fulton, spent some time in his father's business, but was able to retire from business in early middle life. By 1925 he was recognised as having served as a Sunday School teacher for 53 years; he succeeded his father as Church Treasurer in 1888, continuing in that post until the year of his death, 1925. (No one but a Fulton had been Church Treasurer for the first 57 years of the church's existence).

He was for 20 years secretary and treasurer of the Portadown Branch of the NSPCC, and treasurer of the local USPCA. He never sought public office, but did much quiet charitable work. He was much interested in the work of the Salvation Army, contributing to their funds and occasionally presiding at their meetings.

One story sums him up. A stranger called at his house asking his little daughter, who answered the door: "Where is your father?" "I really don't know", was the reply, "but I know he is away doing something for somebody".

W. G. Fulton married Miss Alice Lang, daughter of a Moravian minister, who supported him in his charitable work. Before his death he moved to a house near Belfast – "Alston", between Balmoral and Finaghy, a house that no longer exists.

When William Galway Fulton died on 2nd, December, 1925, Armagh Road had to live, for the first time in its history, without a Fulton. But the life of the Church went on.

Ministry of Rev George Frederick Hampton Wynne, B. A. (1936 - 51)

REV G. F. H. WYNNE, B.A.
Minister 1936 - 51

Mr Wynne was licensed by the Ards Presbytery, and Armagh Road was his first church. He was ordained in Armagh Road on May 28th 1936. On his resignation he went to Seaview Presbyterian Church in 1951, and in 1956 to Great James' Street Church, Londonderry.

Having a new Minister led to discussion on the state of the manse. The general feeling was that the old manse was not worth repairing as a dwelling-house, and in May a sub-committee was appointed to investigate sites for a new one. In any case at that time a retired Minister was legally entitled to retain his manse, and when Mr Perry moved, the letting of the old manse was advertised; it was stated in the advertisement to be suitable for a boarding-house. Later, the Church decided to pay Mr Perry £25 per annum for the use of the manse.

In September 1936, the sub-committee recommended a site in Ridgeway Park "at the rear of Mr Corbett's" for a new manse. This site was bought from Mr Hegan at very favourable terms: 95 feet of frontage at 2/- per foot, when the normal market price was estimated to be 3/9 per foot. Mr Henry was appointed manse architect. In November the Church decided to sell No 1 Tavanagh Terrace, formerly the teacher's residence, to raise money for the Manse Building Fund. On January 28th 1937, an estimate of £1,391-10-0 was accepted from Lyttle & Sons, Carleton Street, and the building proceeded.

When completed the next year, there was a debt of £350-13-1 in the Manse Building Fund.

When the minister had moved out of the Manse, it was possible to make openings from the Academy School, and extend the school premises into the old manse, into what was referred to as the Upper School Room. The school continued to function in these premises until it closed in the nineteen-fifties. Some of our present members began their education here. The school was noted for its football team, and when Mr Don Stevenson was Principal, the Academy team rarely lost a match. Their most famous footballer was Davy Cochrane, one of Northern Ireland's best-ever players.

8 Ridgeway Park North has been the Manse of Armagh Road Church since 1938

In the years leading up to the war, numbers began to increase slowly, though the building of the new manse meant that strict economies were necessary. It was possible to increase Mr Wynne's salary slightly in 1938, to £250 (plus some income from investments).

In early 1939, the Church celebrated its 70th Anniversary. Edenderry Church was having a special collection for a hospital in India, in memory of Rev Alexander Kerr, who had left his ministry in Edenderry almost a century before to work, and die,

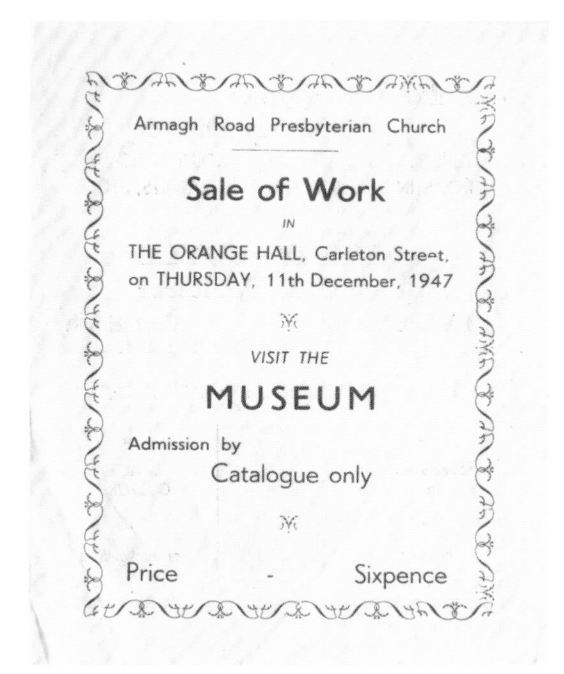

Armagh Road Presbyterian Church

Sale of Work

IN

THE ORANGE HALL, Carleton Street,
on THURSDAY, 11th December, 1947

VISIT THE

MUSEUM

Admission by
Catalogue only

Price - Sixpence

Fundraising, 1947

in the Indian Mission; and Armagh Road decided to give the offerings at its special anniversary services to this fund.

In this year, however, other thoughts often occupied members' minds. War was declared on September 3rd and on September 7th we find the Committee met to discuss the "Blackout". The windows had to be covered with black cloth, and remain so until the danger of air attack had passed, at the end of the war.

Mrs McBride had been appointed organist in 1939, and in 1941 we find record of thanks being expressed to her for her work at the recent Psalm Service, and for her Festival success with the junior choir.

On October 5th 1941, a congregational meeting was held to consider Mr Wynne's request to

Junior BB 1977 – Biggest ever company (with new Manchester City shirts)

be released to serve as a R.A.F. Chaplain. The congregation gave Mr Wynne their approval and best wishes.

Mr Wynne was away until 1946, and during this period assistant Ministers carried on his work. Rev J. S. Woods, B. A., B. D., acted from 1942 to 1945, and Rev H. H. Aitcheson, M. A., from then until Mr Wynne's return.

As the war seemed to be drawing towards an end, it again became possible to plan ahead. A new organ had been needed for some years, and the Committee accepted Mr Herbert Whitten's suggestion that this organ should be a memorial to Mr Perry. In 1945 an Organ Fund was opened and a target of £2,000 was fixed. In that year also the teacher's residence, No 43 Church Street, was sold for £900, after a legal battle about the Church's right to sell it.

In 1946 conditions were returning to normal. A social evening was held on April 16th, the purpose being to present Bibles to 30 members of the

Armagh Road Girl Guide Company Circa 1939.Back row (left to right): M. Gordon, S. Roy, I. Clifford, D. Jones, M. Smart, E. Hynes, J. Dobbin, D. Hollinger. Second Row: M. Martin, D. Conn, J. Swann, M. Robinson, J. Brown, M. Martin, B. Lutton, J. Robinson.Front row: S. Lutton, L. Jenkinson, W. Johnston, Miss D. Espie (Captain), Miss Whiteman (Lt), J. Tipping, N. Waddell, M. Kennedy, M. Cappin.

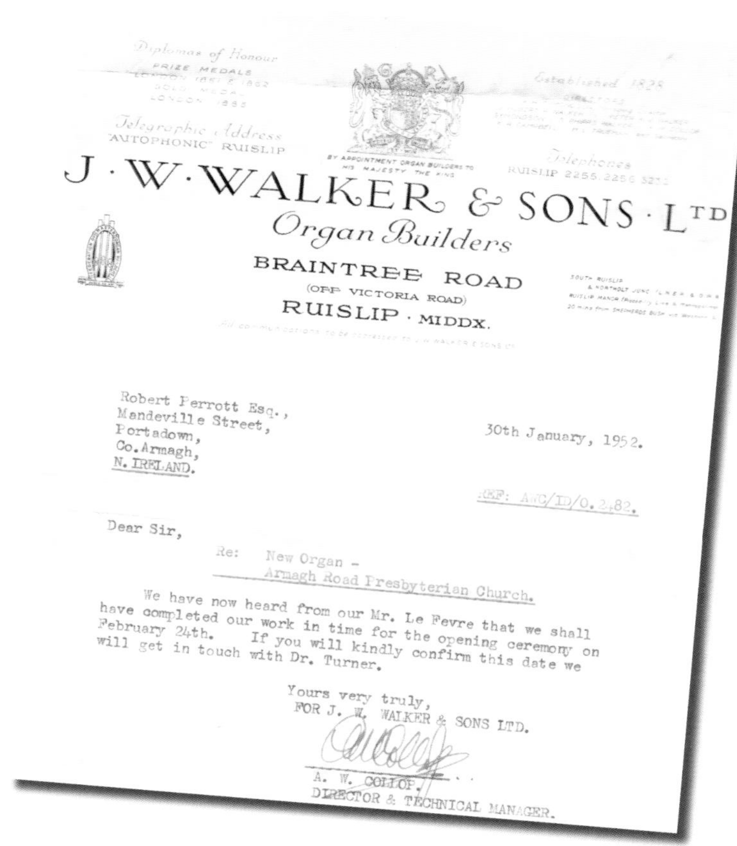
Diplomas of Honour
PRIZE MEDALS
LONDON 1851 & 1862
GOLD MEDAL
LONDON 1885

Telegraphic Address
"AUTOPHONIC" RUISLIP

BY APPOINTMENT ORGAN BUILDERS TO HIS MAJESTY THE KING

Established 1828

Telephones
RUISLIP 2255, 2256

J · W · WALKER & SONS · LTD
Organ Builders
BRAINTREE ROAD
(OFF VICTORIA ROAD)
RUISLIP · MIDDX.

Robert Perrott Esq.,
Mandeville Street,
Portadown,
Co. Armagh,
N. IRELAND.

30th January, 1952.

REF: AWC/ID/O.2482.

Dear Sir,

Re: New Organ -
Armagh Road Presbyterian Church.

We have now heard from our Mr. Le Fevre that we shall have completed our work in time for the opening ceremony on February 24th. If you will kindly confirm this date we will get in touch with Dr. Turner.

Yours very truly,
FOR J. W. WALKER & SONS LTD.

A. W. COLLOP.
DIRECTOR & TECHNICAL MANAGER.

congregation who had served in the Forces. One was collected by the father of a son who, like many other young men, did not come back. Later that year Mr Wynne himself was welcomed back; and the congregation made a presentation to Mr Rowley Patterson who was leaving for the mission field, in South America. A similar gift was made to Mr Fred Swann in 1948, when he left to train for the ministry in Canada.

The names of pew-holders were finally removed at the end of 1946.

The organ was still some way off; but by 1949 members could see a model of it, and an order was placed for a Walker Pipe Organ, at £1,820. This organ was installed and is still in use. In this year the Boys' Brigade was formed and in September the Church held a lively Discussion Night when each organisation had a short time to give its views on church work. The Session was given plenty of ideas to consider.

A significant event was the arrival of Mr Robert Cumming in the Congregation. His talents were soon recognised – he was co-opted to the Session on 3rd, April 1949 and elected Clerk of Session in July 1953.

There were clear signs of growth as Mr Wynne's ministry moved into its last year. The Presbytery Visitation of 1950 praised the greatly improved financial position. Between 1945 and 1950 families increased from 202 to 259, and total income from £656 to £1,380.

Although Mr Wynne resigned in June 1951, his connection with Armagh Road was not yet ended; the new organ was ready before the installation of a new minister, and Mr Wynne was asked to return on February 24th 1952, to dedicate it. This he did, and he also presented a pulpit fall from himself and Mrs Wynne.

Mr Wynne went to Seaview Church and then to Great James' Street, Londonderry. While there he was elected Moderator of the General Assembly in 1975. His work during the rioting in the city in 1968 and later had won him much praise. But Dr Wynne died suddenly on 23rd, July, 1975, after just seven weeks in office, the only Moderator in the history of the Irish Presbyterian Church to die in office. He had been able to visit Armagh Road on 22nd June 1975, and the congratulations which our Church had sent to him had soon to turn to sympathy.

Rev Dr Wynne's son Hampton Wynne was one of the first children to grow up in the Manse. He became a dentist and an elder in Groomsport; but he later performed a service for Armagh Road without realizing it: he introduced Campbell and Louise Wilson to one another.

Ministry of Rev Robert Nesbitt Caswell, B. A., Ph.D. (1952 - 55)

Rev R. N. Caswell, a native of Bangor, was licensed in the Ards Presbytery. (Three of Armagh Road's ministers have come from this Presbytery.)
He was ordained in Third Portglenone Presbyterian Church in 1949, and from there he was called to Armagh Road, where he was installed on February 28th 1952.

ANNOUNCEMENTS.

DATES TO REMEMBER.

SUNDAY February 24th. Dedication of the new pipe organ at the morning Service. Unveiling of Memorials to the late Rev. H. W. Perry, M.A., and Robert Mason, J.P., at the evening service Guest Organist: Dr. T. S. Turner, F.R.C.O.
Rev. G. F. H. Wynne, will conduct the Services.

THURSDAY—February 28th. Installation of Rev. Robert Nesbitt Caswell, B.A., in the Church, at 8 p.m.

FRIDAY—February 29th. Reception to the Rev. R. N. Caswell, B.A., and Mrs. Caswell, in the Christian Workers' Union Hall, Mandeville Street (kindly lent) at 7-30 p.m.

SUNDAY—March 2nd. Opening Services of the New Ministry.
Organist: Miss Marion Hunter.

SUNDAY—March 9th. Services at 11-30 and 7 p.m., conducted by Rev. R. N. Caswell, B.A.
Guest Organist, Mr. R. A. Robb, Organist and Choirmaster of Hill St. Presbyterian Church, Lurgan.

Mr Caswell was awarded the degree of Doctor of Philosophy by Queen's University, Belfast for a thesis entitled "Calvinistic Church Discipline, with special reference to the Church of Scotland". His high reputation as a scholar is indicated by the fact that he was invited to contribute articles on "Excommunication" and "Power of the Keys" to the New Bible Dictionary, published by the Inter-Varsity Fellowship (I.V.F.) in 1962; he was also author of a section of the book "John Calvin", edited by G. E. Duffield and published in 1966.

As a scholar and theologian, Dr Caswell was able to interest members in the principles underlying Presbyterian belief and practice; and his visits to the poorer areas of the town were appreciated. A Mission, conducted by Rev Ivor Lewis, was held during three weeks at the end of 1953. Also in that year six new elders were ordained.

One church member has told the author of how, when he became a Christian and was considering his future career, Dr. Caswell was tireless in helping

Choir Outing in the 1950s, during Rev Dr R. N. Caswell's Time

Back from left to right: Jimmie Palmer, George Gordon, Maureen Williamson, Irene Clifford

3rd row: Lizzie Leeman, Meta Barbour, Ethel Leeman, Eva Spence, Grace Auld, Maisie Smart, Joan Shanks, Dorothy Clifford, Thomas Swann, Norah Hyde, Jim Fenton, Beth Robinson, Marguerite Radcliffe

2nd row: Myrtle Gordon, John Hewitt, Jean Hewitt, Marion Morton, Elaine Perrott

Front row: Jim Smart, George Swann, Stuart Cole (Organist), **Rev R. N. Caswell**, *Gordon Williamson*

him, offering assistance with his educational preparation for possible future Christian work.

In 1953 Miss Marion Hunter resigned as organist, and Mr Stuart Cole took her place. The congregation is very proud to have had the Cole family amongst its members, since the great contribution to missionary work overseas which they have made since then is well-known throughout the Presbyterian Church.

After a ministry of three years Dr Caswell resigned on July 25th 1955, to become Principal of Belfast Bible College. He was then appointed Head of the Religious Education Department at Coleraine Academical Institution, where he spent the remainder of his career. Dr. Caswell still lives in retirement in Belfast.

Christian Endeavour group from 1950's
Back left to right: Norah Hyde, Irene Clifford, Jean Smith, Joan Shanks, Ian Reid.
Front: Maureen Williamson, Gordon Williamson, Joan Monaghan, Maisie Smart, Norman Duncan.

Kirk Session and Congregational Committee held joint meetings in the 1950s

20

Armagh Rd Presbyterian Church.

18th Oct. 1951

Meeting of Session and Committee was held in the Lecture Old Manse at 8 P.M. this eve. Rev. W. H. Craig B.A. B.D. (Edenderry) presiding.

Chairman — Meeting opened with prayer. Members present Mrs Mason Mrs McGaffin

Present — Mrs. E. Leeman Mr J. Nevin J. A. Adams E. Magowan W Kennedy H G McKee W S McCall. G Williamson R Somerville R Herron Secty.

Minutes — Minutes of meeting held in Sept were read approved and signed by the Chairman

Apologies — Apologies for absence was received from Mrs M. Hunter Mr R Cummings R J Hunter.

Thanks — Arising from minutes secty reported permit to carry out alterations in the church had not yet been received from the Ministry of Finance

Reports — Heating of the upper school room would be finished in a short time. It was pro by Mr J A Adams sec by Mrs McGaffin that the thanks and appreciation of the Co. be extended to the Secty and the members who organised and carried through the arrangements of the recent Catering effort. It was decided the profit of £[illegible] made from the effort be allocated to the Organ Fund.

New Manse — The following sub-com were appointed to inspect the Manse in Ridgeway St. and report if decorations are necessary for a new minister coming. Sub com. Mrs R. Mason. H G McKee D. H. W. S. McCall. and Secty

Special Collection — It was decided to have a retiring collection at both services on Remembrance Day Nov. 11th in aid of the Earl Haig Fund. It was also agreed a special appeal be made on behalf of Foreign Missions. And Plate collections at both services on the Foreign Mission Day Services be given to the Fund

Sympathy — It was with very deep regret the Co learned of the death at her residence Warrenpoint of Miss Fulton. A member of a family who in early years took a very keen and practical interest in all the affairs of this church. It was unanimously agreed a wreath be sent on behalf of the Congregation. Mrs R Mason and Mr J. A. Adams expressed their willingness to represent the Cong. at the funeral the following day.

A/c — A/c amounting to £2.13.0 were passed for payment on the pro of Mr W. S. McCall sec by Mrs. E Leeman

Mr Becketts A/c for Church lighting and repairs of £37.

Ministry of Rev William Shaw Magee, B. A., B. D. (1956 - 1979)

Mr Magee was invited to become Armagh Road's sixth Minister in November 1955. Mr Magee was a native of Belfast, and had grown up in Argyll Place Congregation. A serious accident at the age of 16 caused the loss of fingers of his right hand, and ended his career in the butchery business.

He had also been a talented pianist. After spending a summer studying John's Gospel, he decided to train for the ministry, and became assistant to Rev Austin Fulton at St. Enoch's, Belfast. He was then called to Newmills, Co Tyrone in 1949, where he remained until invited to Armagh Road in 1956.

The Magee family

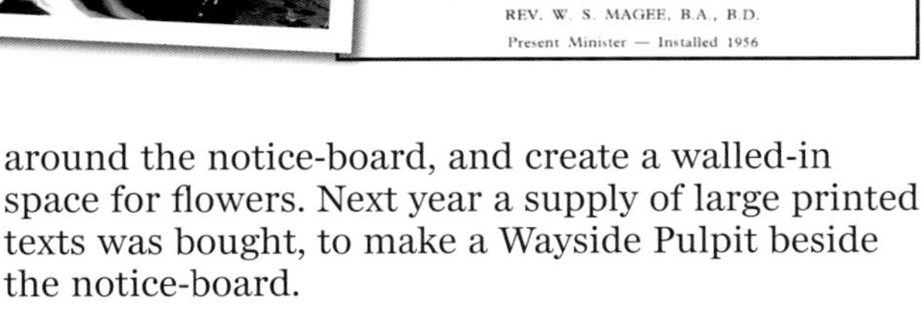

REV. W. S. MAGEE, B.A., B.D.
Present Minister — Installed 1956

He was installed in Armagh Road Church on January 2nd 1956, the reception being held next day in Carleton Street Orange Hall. The practice of carrying in the Bible at the commencement of the Service began shortly afterwards, Mr Magee having explained the symbolic and historic significance of the custom. In September 1956 the Session decided that Communion should be celebrated four times in the year.

In 1956 also, the appearance of the approach to the church changed, when the Committee agreed to remove the shrubs from the front, fill in the area around the notice-board, and create a walled-in space for flowers. Next year a supply of large printed texts was bought, to make a Wayside Pulpit beside the notice-board.

Mr S. Cole, who had been organist, resigned to take up missionary work in Uganda, where he became Principal of a State School. At an earlier date his father, Mr S. Cole (senior), had gone to Kenya to work in Kikuyu prison camps. He has related some of his experiences in a book "Midst Mau Mau". Armagh Road was able to help in the purchase of a Dormobile for his work.

Church Group in 1958: Back left to right: Rev Billy Magee, Sandy Osborne, Billy Irwin, Jimmie Palmer Centre row: Ethel Leeman, Norrie Hunter, Maisie Smart, Jim Houston, Hugh Woolsey, Victor Gordon, Marion Madill, Elaine Perrott, Norah Hyde, Audrey Hill, Eva Radcliffe, Meta Barbour, Irene Clifford, Betty Palmer, Dorothy Clifford, Martha Gordon, Doreen Whitten, Olive Murray, Vionna Murray, Marguerite Radcliffe. Front with teapot: Billy Gordon, Albert Hyde

Towards the end of 1956, Mr R. Cumming was appointed Convenor of a sub-committee to investigate the possibility of building a new Church Hall. The need for such a hall had been obvious for some time; any large meeting had to be held outside the church premises. The Boys' Brigade met in the Temperance Hall, West Street; the reception following Mr Magee's installation was held in the Orange Hall, Carleton Street; and that for Dr Caswell had been held in the Christian Workers' Union Hall, Mandeville Street.

Next year, in September, it was decided to add a new Church Hall to the existing buildings. This, it was hoped, would cost under £7,000. The alternative – to demolish the manse and school-house and build a hall on the same site – would cost, it was estimated, over £10,000, and provide less accommodation.

The hall was built during 1958. The Committee had decided that much of the work could be done

Behold, how good and how pleasant it is for men to work together in unity

Plaque in Church Hall, adapted from Psalm 133 V 1 and recalling the good fellowship during the time of the construction of the hall.

CHRISTIANS TOGETHER
—THE WAY TO LIVE

The only part I have had in the preparation of this brochure is this introduction to it. I am not saying this because I want to dis-own it. What I am saying is that I, like you, have to sit down and examine what it has to say to me as a member of the congregation of Armagh Road.

As I see it, we are not being asked to make any great and dramatic gesture: only to examine the quality of our congregation's life and witness, and the part each of us plays – or ought to play – in it.

The whole point of a congregation is that we are not only christians, but that we are **christians together.** We have to bring up our children in the ways of the people of God, we have to reach out in help to the people about us, and we have to identify ourselves with the Christian Mission in the world at large. These things cannot be done cheaply – and I am not thinking of money alone.

Here we are being asked to consider facts and proposals. Our part is to consider them honestly and in good faith. I am sure that it is in that spirit they are laid before us.

I believe that God's Spirit is prompting us to take a big and courageous step into His future.

WILLIAM S. MAGEE

The Rev. W. S. Magee, B.A., B.D., and Mrs. Magee pictured at home with their six children John, James, David, Heather, Elizabeth and Ruth.

Outreach in 1963 encouraging people to examine the quality of their church and faith life

In the early 1960s the Church was having a sponsored slim to raise funds to finance the new Church Hall. To promote the event Rev Magee had his waist measured together with Bob Fenton (left) and John Hunter. Holding the tape measure are twins Margaret (left) and Elizabeth Murdock Photo: Victor Gordon

by voluntary labour. In February, Mr W. F. Gordon was given full responsibility for organizing and supervising the work, and by December 11th of the same year, the building was complete and the opening ceremony was performed appropriately by Mrs Gordon.

The cost of the work, including alterations to the old manse and school-house, was £7,500. This amount would have been very much greater but for the fact that a number of the men of the congregation did the main part of the work by voluntary labour.

Hanging in the hall is an inscription, bearing words adapted from the first verse of Psalm 133: "Behold how good and how pleasant it is for brethren to work together in unity". The benefits were not simply the work done and the money saved, but the sense of fellowship which working together created.

To perpetuate this, a Men's Fellowship was formed, and in subsequent years both the spiritual and material life of the congregation gained. The men carried out work which saved the church many thousands of pounds; and the Fellowship also figured largely in the promotion of other projects for the benefit of the Church, among them being the rewiring of the church, the purchase of carpets for the church, and the obtaining and improvement of a cottage in the Mournes for the use of youth groups, etc. It is not accidental that visiting ministers later commented on the high proportion of men attending church in Armagh Road.

Kenneth McCall's Youth Fellowship on a treasure hunt by bicycle in summer 1960. The day ended in 'Sausage Sizzle' in Mr Cumming's Garage

60 years 2nd Portadown BB Company (1949 - 2009). Michael Wilson, Captain for the past 10 years

BB training for Duke of Edinburgh Award in 2006 - John Smart, Jake Mercer, Craig Patterson and David Meek

Ordination of new elders March 1961

Back Row: Robert Cumming, George Swann, Joseph Thornton, Front: William Belshaw, James Houston, Rev W S Magee, William D F Irwin, John Moore

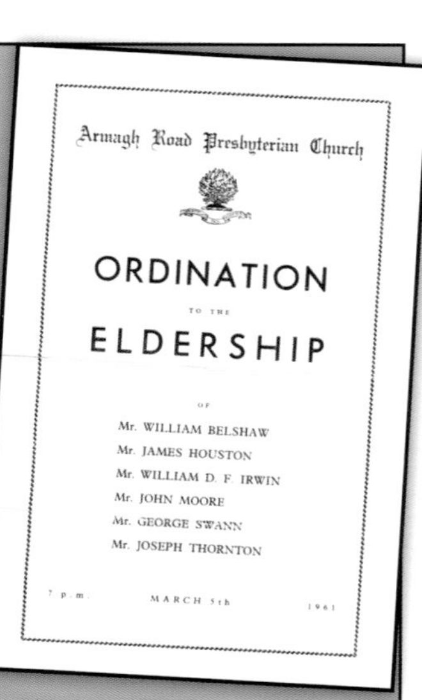

Armagh Road Presbyterian Church

ORDINATION

TO THE

ELDERSHIP

OF

Mr. WILLIAM BELSHAW
Mr. JAMES HOUSTON
Mr. WILLIAM D. F. IRWIN
Mr. JOHN MOORE
Mr. GEORGE SWANN
Mr. JOSEPH THORNTON

7 p.m. MARCH 5th 1961

On the stage of Armagh Road Church Hall: Member of Session Mr W. Irwin hands over the keys to the surprised new car owners William and Mona Magee

One person in particular helped most generously with the church's work in this and subsequent years – Mr W. D. F. Irwin. When, in early 1967, the Committee had the sad duty of recording his death, they wrote in a Memorial Minute: "Almost every corner of our premises reveals some token of his generosity and interest. His gifts to this congregation amounted to thousands of pounds, given anonymously or hidden within some current project. He was a humble, brotherly man who enjoyed the company of his fellows from all walks of life without distinction."

On August 18th 1957 Armagh Road began a new chapter in its activities; for this was the date of its first radio broadcast. Since that evening service, the church has been on the air more that two dozen times. In addition, Mr Magee had many other studio broadcasts on radio and television; and in 1967 a service in Armagh Road was televised for the first time.

How ARPC got their broadcasting minister speechless? They asked him to organise a meeting without letting him know what for. Hidden behind the curtain of the stage was a special gift to enable him get around the congregation.

Broadcasting was regarded by the congregation not as an opportunity to perform party pieces, but as an opportunity to spread the Gospel in a wider field. It has the same motives as those which took Rev James and Mrs McCammon to Manchuria, Fred Swann to Canada, the Cole family to Africa, Joy Logan to Israel and Jamaica, Norman Duncan to India, Rowley Patterson to mission work in Ireland and South America.

Steven Bamford in Kenya in Summer 2008

Outreach from Armagh Road Church still continues in the 21st century: In 2008 Claire Shepherd in Cameroon with Wycliffe Bible Translating Society

The Church at the Reformation used the new means of communication – printing – to bring its message to people's attention; and Mr Magee and his congregation were convinced that the Church today must be equally alert to the possibilities of modern means of communication – radio and television. Religious broadcasting then had greater prominence than it has today.

The Light Programme People's Service (of which Armagh Road had several) had an audience of four million. And when television became common, there were services and epilogues on BBC and ITV channels. All of this required much work by the Minister and choir. The broadcasts brought in numerous letters from listeners, and all of them were answered by the Minister.

Mr R. A. Robb was organist 1930 - 38 and again 1957-65, and the success of the broadcasts owed much to him. On radio particularly, the quality of the music is of great importance, and Mr Robb raised the performance of the choir to a level few choirs of its size could equal.

In 1971 Rodney Spence was appointed organist. It was one of the Church's best appointments; Rodney is still there, and the standard of music became if anything even higher.

Mr Magee's conversational style was particularly suited to broadcasting, and his interest in broadcasting helped the wider church.

From 1963 to 1973 he was Convener of the TV and Broadcasting Committee of the Presbyterian Church, and in 1979 he was elected to the joint BBC/ITV National Committee for Religious Broadcasting.

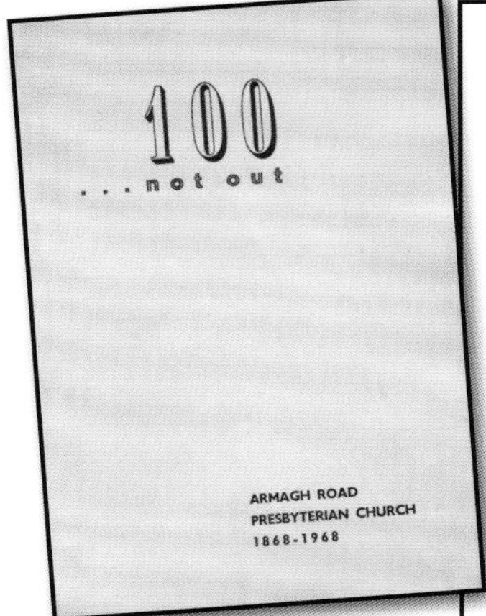

100
. . . not out
ARMAGH ROAD
PRESBYTERIAN CHURCH
1868-1968

Centenary Service 1969
(from: Portadown News)

Postscript

by REV. W. S. MAGEE, B.A., B.D.

As the present minister of Armagh Road I wish to express my appreciation of this lively history of the congregation written by Mr. Mervyn Gilmour, one of our elders. He is to be congratulated on his work.

It is obvious that for many years the congregation was weak numerically and financially. The struggle was long and hard. It is equally obvious that there have always been devoted people ready to spend and be spent. We have entered into a heritage made possible under God by their faithfulness. Some of these people are still with us and we rejoice in the fact.

We are riding high now. We ought to be warned. Perhaps there will be more perils in our future than in our past. It will be no easier to keep the faith amid the "progress" of our times than it was for men who knew nothing of our comforts or our affluence. We can feel already contrary winds and tides.

At this time we rightly give thanks for the past and for our present good estate. This, however, is no guarantee of our future. Our future rests in God's gracious will. For the Church of Jesus Christ does not exist "by the will of the flesh or the will of man, but of God". As one hundred years ago men began this work in faith so we will continue.

"We come unto our fathers' God. Their God is our salvation".

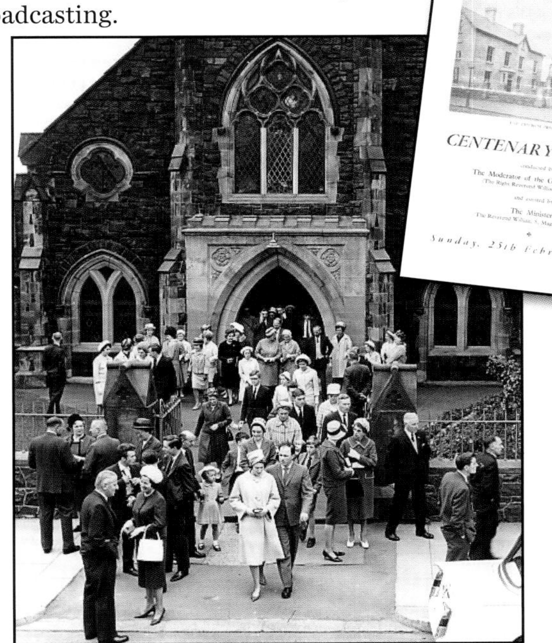

Armagh Road Presbyterian Church
1868 - 1968
CENTENARY SERVICE
The Moderator of the General Assembly
The Minister
Sunday, 25th February, 1968

Centenary Service 1968 (from: Portadown News)

When the Church celebrated its centenary in 1968, a short history was published entitled "100 Not Out". Mr Magee in his postscript warned against complacency:

"We are riding high now. We ought to be warned. Perhaps there will be more perils in our future than in our past. It will be no easier to keep the faith amid the 'progress' of our times than it was for men who knew nothing of our comforts or our affluence. We can feel already contrary winds and tides.

"At this time we rightly give thanks for the past and for our present good estate. This, however, is no guarantee of our future. Our future rests in God's gracious will. For the Church of Jesus Christ does not exist 'by the will of the flesh or the will of men, but of God'. As one hundred years ago men began this work in faith so we will continue.

"We come unto our fathers' God. Their God is our salvation".

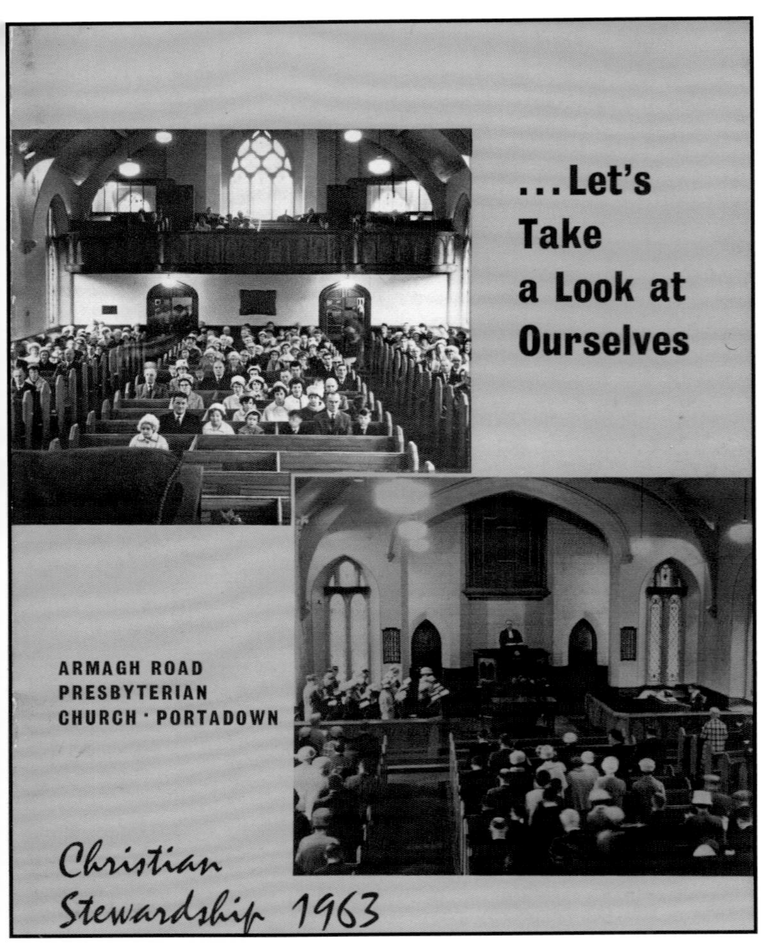

...Let's
Take
a Look at
Ourselves
ARMAGH ROAD
PRESBYTERIAN
CHURCH · PORTADOWN
Christian
Stewardship 1963

Christian Stewardship Outreach project 1963 – A View on the Congregation from the Pulpit and Gallery Prospective

Kenneth McCall's Youth Fellowship – 1960s

Mr Magee was right. Soon after 1968, difficult times came to Portadown. Violence became common; Church members were killed, and families lost members who are still remembered. The Church was particularly shocked by the cowardly murder of a highly regarded elder, Walker Whitten, in 1977.

Anchor Boys around 1970 with leaders Betty Wilson and Mavis McCallum

Financially and statistically Armagh Road was doing well in the 1960s and 1970s. Numbers at Communion Services reached 235, and the church was able to give large amounts to Church Extension and Missions.

Mr Magee was a profound thinker. Not everyone could follow the depths of his thought, but he normally included in his services an address for the young teenagers, and that provided sustenance for some who found the main sermon difficult.

But in 1979 it became clear that Mr Magee's health was failing. When it became known that his condition was terminal, one lady told the author that she cried for a week. He died on 23rd December 1979. His friend Rev Moore Wasson had recently retired from the BBC, and was able to help greatly in the congregation in late 1979 and during the vacancy.

When Mr Magee died, the Moderator of the General Assembly was Rev Dr W. M. Craig, the much respected minister of our sister church, First Portadown. Dr Craig spoke warmly of Mr Magee's commitment to modern methods of communication, and of his willingness to share his expertise with his fellow Ministers.

2nd Portadown Junior BB – Battalion Football Cup Winners 1978
Back Row: Ian Quinn, Mark Jackson, Derek Moore, Ian Sergeant, Mark Armstrong, Mark Swann, Philip Woolsey. Front Row: Michael McCaughey, Wayne Pearson, Ian Jackson, Jeffrey Armstrong, John Smart, Derek Magill, John Hawkins

SERVICE OF THANKSGIVING
FOR THE LIFE OF
The
Reverend William S. Magee, B.A., B.D.,
3 p.m. Sunday 20th January 1980
IN
Armagh Road Presbyterian Church

Cover of Thanksgiving Service for Rev William S. Magee

Service of Ordination of new Elders with Presbytery Commission Rev J C M Anderson, Moderator and Rev A R Scott, Clerk and their representative elders on 16 September 1979: Rev Jim Harrison, James McBain, Victor Gordon, Leonard Moles, Geo Jackson, Thelma Jackson, James Magee, Sam Paul, Olive Smart, David Pepper, Bob Muldrew, Bob Cumming, Rev J C M Anderson, Rev William Magee

Ministry of Rev Campbell Wilson (1980 - 2004)

Rev F. A. C. Wilson came from the Garvagh area, and after a time as assistant in McQuiston Congregation he was called to Tullylish, County Down.

His fame had spread to Portadown, and he was called to Armagh Road remarkably quickly – he was installed on 20th June 1980, just under six months after Mr Magee's death.

Campbell and Louise Wilson with their children Elaine, Paul, Christopher and Duncan

Meet the Wilson family

IT WILL take time for the Rev. Campbell Wilson to meet – and to get to know – all the members of the congregation and vice versa.

But in order to give the congregation a head-start, 'Contact' is introducing the Rev. Wilson, his wife Louise and their four children – Paul (9), Duncan (7), Elaine (6), and Christopher (2).

The Rev. Campbell Wilson hails from between Coleraine and Garvagh, he is the son of a grocer, and his 'home' church is First Garvagh Presbyterian.

He is a former pupil of Coleraine Inst., went on to study at Magee College, Londonderry, Trinity College, Dublin and Assembly's College. He gained his M.A. degree at Trinity.

Mr. Wilson's first call was to Mc. Quiston Memorial in Belfast, where he was assistant minister from 1969-72. Then he was minister at Tullylish, Banbridge from 1972-1980.

BANGOR

Mrs. Louise Wilson is from Bangor, and she, too, is a born-and-bred Presbyterian – First Bangor is her 'home' Church.

She was educated at Bangor Technical College and worked as a dental secretary at the Royal Victoria Hospital.

A dentist at 'The Royal' introduced the couple. That dentist was Hampton Wynne, son of the late Rev. George Wynne, former minister here in Armagh Road.

They were married at Assembly's College in May 1970 – Mrs. Wilson's minister was on holiday at the time, so Professor Barcley, principal at Assembly's performed the ceremony.

The Armagh Road youth leaders are delighted that there are four children in the Wilson family – especially the B.B. with three boys!

Paul and Duncan are already keen members of the Junior B.B., while Elaine has joined the Bunnies. All three are well settled into their new school – Millington Primary.

Christopher will be most welcome at the Robins in a couple of years. Right now, he enjoys the creche each Sunday morning – after a rather noisy start!

The Rev. and Mrs. Wilson with their children – from left – Duncan, Christopher, Elaine and Paul.

1980 – James Magee presenting Pulpit fall on behalf of Mrs Mona Magee and in Memory of the late Rev Billy Magee to the Rev Campbell Wilson and Armagh Road Church. From l – r: Robert Cumming, Rev Dr Austin Fulton, Rev Campbell Wilson, James Magee, Rev Dr William Craig, Tom Forbes

On 10th November 1980 the Session recorded its thanks to the Magee family for the gifts of a Pulpit Fall and desk in memory of their father Rev W. S. Magee. Then on 2nd October 1983 there were similar thanks for a set of three Communion trays with cups presented by Mr James Magee on behalf of his mother Mrs Mona Magee. On 18th March 1984 eight Communion chairs were presented by Mrs Mary B. Irwin in memory of Mr W. D. F. Irwin.

Young Wives – Young Women's Group celebrating 21st Birthday

Second row l – r: Myriel Black, Ena Osborne, Maisie Smart, Pat Rogerson, Lillian Ramsay, Rosemary Graham, Sandra Wright

Front l-r: Elaine Irwin, Ingrid Dalzell, Louise Wilson, Olive Smart, Freda Brown, Shirley Swann

Visit of Moderator 1992, The Right Rev Dr John Dunlop with ARPC Elders: (l–r) Bob Cumming, William Irwin, Olive Smart, John Bradfield, Ellis Gaw, Rosemary McCall, Bertie Dalzell, Hugh Woolsey, Errol Whitten, Rev Campbell Wilson, Dessie Rainey, Noel Greenlee, Dr John Dunlop, Sandy Osborne, Mervyn Gilmour, Betty Wilson, Bertie Anderson, Jim Smart, Thelma Jackson, Sam Paul, Billy Jackson, Daphne Gilmour, Bill Dickey, Alec Edgar, George Miskimmins, Josh Liggett, John McKibben, and Victor Gordon

Mr Wilson soon became a well-liked Minister, particularly popular with children and young people. He was always supported by his wife Louise, who was able not only to raise a family of four children but to play an active part in the life of the congregation, and to be a valued member of the church choir.

Mr Wilson's early years in Portadown coincided with much violence in the town. Large bombs destroyed much of the town centre, and expressions of hatred were widespread. Mr Wilson worked hard to promote good will and understanding in the town, speaking out fearlessly against intolerance. It was noticeable that groups which needed a hall for cross-community meetings often turned to Armagh Road for accommodation.

ARPC Brownies 1980: with (from left top right) Tawny Owl Irene McKee and Officer Jane Smart and Brown Owl Heather Beggs

Through these years the congregation owed much to Mr Robert Cumming, who was Clerk of Session from 1953 to 1989. Mr Cumming had been ordained Elder in 1942 in Kirkpatrick Memorial Congregation in Belfast (where he also played football for Dundela).

He came to Portadown in 1947, where his leadership qualities were soon recognised. He was soon co-opted to the Session, and elected Clerk of Session in 1949. That same year he founded the Boys' Brigade Company, of which he was Captain for the next 15 years. He was also Sunday School Superintendent for 21 years. Outside of his work for the Congregation he used his professional knowledge and skills to assist in the major refurbishment of Church House in Belfast. For that work he was created an Elder of the General Assembly, a rare honour. Mr Cumming retired as Clerk on 10th April 1989, after 36 years in that post, and died on 27th June 1997. His dynamic service to the Congregation for 50 years has been unequalled.

Mr Cumming was succeeded as Clerk by Mr Billy Jackson, whose friendly manner made him popular with everyone. He had always been a hard worker in the Church and this has continued to the present day. Mr Jackson remained Clerk until 1997, when he was succeeded by Miss Daphne Gilmour, who had been the Congregation's first woman Elder, and who was its first woman Clerk.

First Lady Clerk of Kirk Session in Portadown and Presbytery of Armagh

Daphne Gilmour representing PCI in the Civic Forum

Daphne was active in many areas of Church life. She was elected to the Central Executive of the World Alliance of Reformed Churches, and represented the Presbyterian Church in such places as Sao Paolo, Seoul and Geneva.

Junior BB after having won the Battalion Figure Marching Cup 1985 with Warrant Officer Eliz Gordon and Lieutenant Ivan Stirling

TIMES, SEPTEMBER 19, 1997

...om the churches...News from the church...

Armagh Road appoints lady clerk

ARMAGH Road Presbyterian Church has elected the first lady Clerk of Session in its 130-year history.

Miss Daphne Gilmour was unanimously chosen at the church's September session meeting on Monday night and succeeds Mr William Jackson who has held the post for seven years.

Miss Gilmour is Religious Education Adviser to the Southern Education and Library Board, and before that was Head of RE at Portadown College.

She is a former student of the school and taught there for 13 years after holding number of teaching positions.

For seven years she has been the Presbyterian Church in Ireland's sole representative to the World Alliance of Reformed Churches, a post which took her to Hungary, North America and the Far East.

Miss Gilmour brother, Mr Mervyn Gilmour, is also an elder at Armagh Road where they have worshipped for some 30 years after moving into Portadown from their home T[illegible]aghan area.

She has con[illegible] religious b[illegible] from time to time, notably on BBC Radio Ulster's 'Thought for the Day' morning slot, and is widely respected within the Presbyterian Church in Ireland.

Daphne elected

Miss Daphne Gilmour - new Clerk of Session at Armagh Road Presbyterian Church. 38-201.

The Rev Campbell Wilson, minister at Armagh Road, paid tribute to the work of William Jackson for his work as Clerk of Session.

"He has been a tremendous worker," said Mr Wilson. "But Daphne will be a worthy successor."

Miss Daphne Gilmour – First Lady Clerk of Kirk Session in Portadown and Presbytery of Armagh

When Daphne had to retire because of ill health in 2002, her brother Mervyn was elected to succeed her. When he retired in 2007, he was succeeded by Ivan Stirling.

Rev Campbell Wilson was invited to spend some weeks at the Highlands Church in North Carolina, at a time when Americans were anxious to understand what was going on in Northern Ireland.

There had been a number of discussions over the years on the best time for commencing the morning service, and on 26th September 1993 a Congregational meeting decided to move the time from 11.30 am to 11.00 am, by 149 votes to 73.

Efforts to improve the church have continued. In 1999 two plaques were installed inside the church as memorials to Rev W. S. Magee and to Mr Robert Cumming. In the same year Pew Bibles were dedicated, the gift of the McConnell family in memory of Mrs Orr-McCauley.

In the same spirit, during the ministry of Rev C. Bradley, in 2005 a set of the new Irish Presbyterian Hymnbook was presented by the Reid family in memory of a popular member, Mr Billy Reid, who had died suddenly.

The organisations of the church have continued to provide fellowship for members and to attract devoted service. The Boys' Brigade celebrated its 50th anniversary with a special service on 17th October 1999. This was a remarkable event, drawing back former members from several countries, even one from Canada; and showing how boys had valued the work of leaders down the years. It was very appropriate that the service was conducted by a former member of the Company, Rev Donald Patton, soon to be Moderator of the General Assembly. In recent years the Boys Brigade, and youth work generally, has owed much to Mr Michael Wilson.

For the girls of the congregation the Girl Guides have provided a similar function, and have also attracted devoted leadership. Mrs Phyllis Jeffers became a leader as soon as she could legally, at age 18. Next year she has to retire at age 65, so she has completed 46 years as leader! Her colleague as leader, Mrs Alison Courtney, has completed 36 years. The Guides have often participated in national and international events, and they are proud of the fact that in 1983 Ruth Muldrew was selected, out of the whole United Kingdom, to present a copy of the New Guide Handbook to Princess Margaret.

Visit of the Right Rev Dr Trevor Morrow Moderator in 2000. 2nd row: Daphne Gilmour, Iris McAllister, Mrs Carys Morrow, Rev Campbell Wilson, Dr Trevor Morrow. Front row: Jason and Samantha Adams, Jessica and Emily McDonald, and Keith Adams

The Bowling Club has not only provided fellowship for many members, but has also given generously to church funds. The Sales and Auctions organised by Mr George Swann have been a feature of church life for many years. There always seems to have been a devoted band of practical men and women who do much to keep the property clean and in good repair. Now this is often effected through the Property Sub-committee.

The excellence of the Choir has already been mentioned. In 1971 the church was waiting for Rodney Spence to graduate from Queen's University,

Candle Light Christmas Service before the redecoration of the Church with Rev Campbell Wilson in the pulpit

so that he could take up the post of organist and choirmaster; and at the time of the writing of this book, he is still there! All through these years the standard of music has been very high. The special Services at Harvest and Christmas have been memorable, but on the ordinary Sundays inspiration is always present. Talented individuals have contributed much. Anna McKeag and Deborah McDonald have provided solo parts; Ronnie Bothwell, a remarkable flautist, is an asset to the worship of any Congregation. And Victor Gordon has now sung at 53 consecutive Harvests!

When long service is mentioned, it should be recorded that on September 19th 1979, Mr John Bradfield was appointed Permanent Member of the Vestibule Rota; and he has been greeting visitors, and members, ever since.

Mr Wilson was an active and energetic man, but in mid career he had to deal with the challenging fact that he was suffering from Multiple Sclerosis. Gradually he became unable to move freely, to drive a car, to write, and to do so many of the things that made his life and ministry rewarding and enjoyable.

But the way in which he dealt with these problems was a ministry in itself. He travelled around the town in a series of special vehicles, and in doing so he became the best-known Minister in the town.

Others who had similar problems have testified that he has been an inspiration to them, showing that life can be productive and rewarding despite difficulties. Those who have experienced his practical and inspiring preaching have felt that if they had only heard his message over a loudspeaker, they would never have guessed that he worked under such difficulties.

Mr Wilson's fellow ministers in the Presbytery and Assembly did what they could to help. From 1993 Miss Carol McRoberts worked as a Deaconess in the Congregation for a three year period.

Rev Walter Herron, a retired Minister, worked in the Congregation from 1996 to 2002, providing pastoral assistance. He stopped, aged 80, only because he was no longer allowed to drive, and was given a well-deserved presentation. Other retired Ministers helped by conducting Evening Services.

On 19 April 2004 Mr Wilson announced that he was demitting his charge with effect from 30 June 2004. A farewell evening was organised, at which many spoke of what they had gained from his ministry, and of their great affection for Mrs Louise Wilson.

Something which gave Mr Wilson great pleasure was the collection of cards which he received from people in Great Britain and further afield, who had been children and young people under his ministry, and who remembered him warmly.

During the vacancy the congregation was indebted to the Ministers in charge of the vacancy, Rev Stephan van Os and Rev Ann McDonald.

Ministry of Rev Christina Bradley (2005 -)

During the vacancy the attention of the Congregation's Hearing Committee gradually focused on Rev Christina Bradley. She was elected Minister at a Congregational Meeting on 9th May 2005, was installed by the Armagh Presbytery on 15th June, and commenced her ministry on 19th June 2005. The Choir had excelled itself in greeting her by singing Luther's hymn "Ein' feste Burg" in German!

Photo: Doris Steinborn

Mrs Bradley is the first Minister from outside Northern Ireland, and the first woman Minister, in the history of the Congregation. She was born in Eastern Germany, and studied at various Universities, mainly the University of Tübingen, but also at Vienna, Hamburg and Edinburgh.

After ordination in 1983 and work in parishes of Lutheran Confession in Southern Germany, she came to Northern Ireland in 1999. The 2001 General Assembly received her as a Minister of the Presbyterian Church in Ireland.

During her first year as Assistant Minister in Belfast she attended Union Theological College, Belfast, for further studies on the history of the Presbyterian Church in Ireland and The Westminster Confession.

Rev Bradley worked as Ordained Assistant to V Rev Dr John Dunlop in Rosemary Presbyterian Church Belfast, from which she was called to Armagh Road.

19th June 2005 – The newly installed Minister with members of her family: Cristina Beatriz De la Rosa, Manfred O. C. Kirschner, Christina U. Bradley, Jim Bradley, Katie A Bradley, Nan Bradley, Rosane Frida De la Rosa and Michael Kirschner

September 2008: The Right Rev Dr Donald Patton, a former member of Armagh Road Church, visits the congregation of his childhood again, now as Moderator of The General Assembly. Pictured are at the back: Alec Edgar, Ivan Stirling (Clerk of Session), David Lowry, Errol Whitten, Ivan Connor, John Bradfield, Betty Wilson, George Swann, John Kilner, Dr William Ramsay. At the front: Victor Gordon, Dessie Rainey, Carlo Hughes, Billy Jackson, Moyra Stirling, Mrs Florence Patton, Dr Donald Patton, Rev Christina Bradley, Thelma Jackson, Ellis Gaw, Rosemary McCall *Photo Ellis Gaw*

ARPC Choir with Choir Master and Organist Rodney Spence and Rev C. Bradley. Back Row: Arnold Hatch, Victor Gordon, Wilfie Moore, Mitchell Graham, Rodney Spence. Middle Row: Rosemary Graham, Isabel Orr, Jim Smart, Ronnie Bothwell, Ellis Gaw. Front Row: Viola Millar, Betty Wilson, Anne Lowry, Rev Christina Bradley

Her ministry has been marked by use of drama and the arts, and much imaginative work with children, and careful pastoral work with the sick and the bereaved. This should pay dividends in the future.

All histories have to end somewhere, and this seems a suitable place to end this one. The congregation looks forward to the years ahead, fortified by memories of the devoted service of so many people in the years which have passed.

Mervyn D Gilmour

Postscript

by Rev Christina U. R. Bradley

Sunday School Superintendent Moyra Stirling among the Youth Church and Sunday School children on Children's Sunday in June 2008. Front Row from l - r: Sarah Nelson, Lauren Buckley, Erin Buckley, Moyra Stirling, Rachel Bamford, Andrew Berry, Alice Berry, Louise Meek. Next row back from l - r: Mary Shilliday with Robbie, Maureen Maguire, Anna-Louise Shepherd, Ben Shepherd, David Meek, Lara Nelson with Molly Nelson.
Second row back: Teddy Mason, Manfred Kirschner, Agnes Thornton

With every second, yes indeed each new morning and evening, time moves on. Once the night is past a new day lies ahead. With it come good times and bad, and amid tears and laughter we pass from one generation to the next. Birthdays and centenaries are looked upon as special days to be celebrated in style ... yet, does any moment or day ever return?

In our congregation this year, 2009, is an opportunity for celebrating 140 years of the Church building we own (with 2008 already marking the 140th year since the foundation of Second Portadown Presbyterian Church), 60 years of having a pipe organ and the 60th year of Second Portadown BB Company with Anchor Boys, Junior BB and BB Company section. BB Captains have come and gone, likewise ministers and leaders of organisations. Only the Church is still the same; and members of Armagh Road Church are aware that within the twinkling of an eye what happened yesterday is history today.

When we celebrated the 140th Church Anniversary on 29th March 2009 I greeted the congregation on the Order of Service with these words:

"A very warm welcome to you this morning! Enjoy this day which God has made to give you a break from all your work. Today we continue to celebrate the birth of Armagh Road Church as a result of people listening to God's word and yearning for a place of worship nearer their homes in 1868. The Church building and all the premises we have now we owe to the initiative and generosity of people who came before us. So we praise God for his keeping and guidance over all those years and pray for his grace and peace to be with us in all that lies ahead."

140th Anniversary of Armagh Road Church Building

(141st of the foundation of the congregation)

These are the people – and there are many more that happened not to be in the focus of the camera – who celebrated the 140th Birthday of Armagh Road Church.

140th Anniversary of Armagh Road Presbyterian Church Birthday Cake

Cutting the Birthday Cake for the 140th Birthday of Armagh Road Presbyterian Church: Anna Hughes, Alice Berry, Andrew Berry, Beth Moates, Rev C. U. R. Bradley and Harry Hughes

Rev C. U. R. Bradley thanks Rev Dr David Lapsley from Belfast, and his wife Vicky, for preaching and celebrating with ARPC at the 140th Church Anniversary

Sammy Jones, John Bradfield, Sammy's Brother Albert Jones, Mervyn Gilmour, Alana Meek

L-r: Herbert and Frances McComisky, Eileen Greenlee, Heather and Molly Moates, Noel Greenlee

Mable Anderson, June Millar, Bertha Brown, William Hughes, Sandra Hughes, Gerry Brown and Tommy Anderson's left ear

Deirdre Kilner, John Kilner, Caroline McCall, Rosemary McCall, Sam Paul, Billy Jackson, Viola Millar

Betty Wilson, Shirley Swann, Dawn Conner, Isabel Orr serving at the 140th Anniversary Lunch after Church

But who are the men, women and children that came before us? Who are those who generously gave of their time and money so that the congregation would have a home for meeting and prayer today, tomorrow and in times to come?

In reading Mervyn Gilmour's History of Armagh Road Presbyterian Church and looking at the photographs and images of the past, many of those who worshipped in this church since its foundation will come alive again. We can detect a great sense of humour in the congregation. Presbyterians are at times known for being serious and serene. But Mervyn's words reveal this congregation to be full of fun and laughter, a surprising bunch of people.

Each of these photographs is but a spotlight focusing on a moment in time of a rich church life. We experience births and deaths, there are Services

Not doing what her Minister says: "Ann, clap your hands!" Ann Paul is not prepared to clap her hands just yet!

Matthew F. J. Gamble with parents Ashleigh and Nicholas Gamble after Emergency Baptism in Craigavon Hospital on 1st September 2009

of Thanksgiving and Church Weddings. Times of celebration and socialising are interspersed with work in Kirk Session and Congregational Committee meetings; and there are Baptisms of children, young people and adults, but also the confirmation of Faith and Baptism when members become Communicant members.

However things in life don't always go as planned; the sudden illness of a new born baby makes young parents and their families anxious for the life of the baby. These are days of trial and tribulations, days between hope and desperation. This is where faith and prayer come in at the deep end ...

Doctors and nurses don't automatically have it in their hands to see their patients recover. But, when a baby gets well again, as did little Matthew, there is that feeling of gratitude and praise to God for His goodness and keeping. This is an awesome experience - turning tears into laughter. And so thankfulness in everything changes all things and opens new ways of looking at life.

After Baptism the congregation makes a promise before God. For children who received Emergency Baptism at hospital, the congregation will make the same promise in church at a later stage, when the youngster is well enough to be brought to church again. The promise to be made for Matthew is this:

"Matthew, for YOU Jesus Christ came into the world, for you he was baptised, for you he died on Calvary and cried at the last: 'it is accomplished'! For you he triumphed over death, for you he rose in newness of life and ascended to reign at God's right hand. All this he did for you, Matthew, though you do not know it yet, but - with God's help - we will tell you of all these things."

And so our Christian faith has been passed on for almost a century and a half. Our mission as a local Church in Portadown is to live our faith in such a way that all who meet us sense the love of God, the grace of Jesus and the compassion of the Holy Spirit in our midst. A life of love is at the heart of a welcoming church where men, women and especially children and vulnerable people feel welcome, safe and at home.

Irish Inter-Church Band with musicians from St John the Baptist and Armagh Road Church: from l – r: Eunan McCreesh, John Bradfield, Aine McCreesh-West and Jim Smart

Back row: Tommy Anderson, Sam Paul, Ivan Stirling, Billy Jackson, Teddy Mason and John McKibben.
Front row: Included are, Sam Crory, Ryan Crory, Harry Hughes, Anne Paul, Jennifer Hughes and to the right Gretta Marks and Lara Nelson

There are many gifts and skills in this congregation. Some are shared with the people of the Church: think of music and song or things some people can do with their hands. Art and craft, wood work and painting come to mind; but also building,

Country Comes to Town 2007 – BBQ outside ARPC – Steven Bamford, Alison Magee, James Bamford and David O'Neill serving the public

tiling, laying carpets and decorating, building furniture, cooking delicious dishes, managing the sound system or playing musical instruments.

Other gifts and skills are lived and realised outside church, at different workplaces or times of leisure as God created each and every human being with all sorts of gifts and abilities to develop the skills that make a person unique and special in his or her ways.

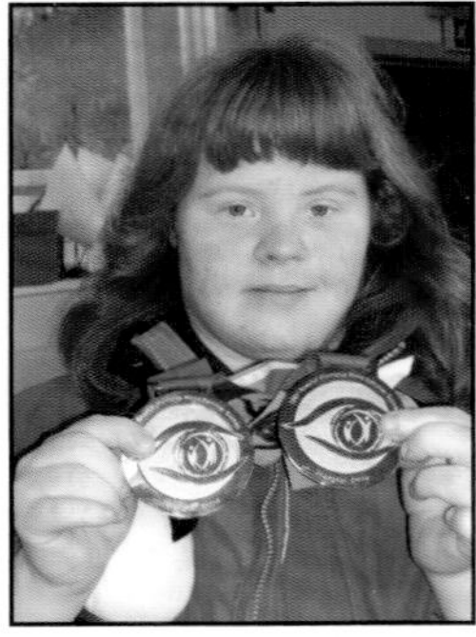

Carol and Ruth Swann in China at the 2007 Special Olympics World Summer Games in Shanghai: Ruth Swann one of our young people, won two Silver Medals for Ireland in the discipline of swimming Butterfly and Front Crawl

L - R: Ena Osborne, Alec Edgar, Mildred Heslip, Andy Millar, Terry Millar, Sidney Conn

November 2009 Clothes Collection for fundraising. L - R: Ivan Conner, Dr David Lowry, Errol Whitten and John Adams

The children and young people of our Church are not merely our future: they are our today and thus our tomorrow. If God wills, they will be writing our continuing history later on.

During "Children's Special" in Church on 1st Advent 2009 up at the front of the Church: Back l-r: Rhys Heasty, Dylan Heasty, Sophie and Michelle Montgomery, Bradley Stuart. Front l-r: Becky and Craig Anderson, Molly Heatrick.

Killowen Outdoor Activity Weekend, February 2008. Back, among others: James O'Neill, Craig Patterson, Gavin Steele, William Robb, Ben Shepherd. Front: Jake Mercer, David Meek, Wilfred Steele, Moyra Stirling, Louise Meek, Ann-Louise Shepherd, Rachael Bamford, Ruth Stirling and Sarah Jennings

During "Children's Special" in Church on 1st Advent 2009. Stuart Shilliday, Andrew Berry, Harry Hughes, Anna Hughes, Annie Gordon, Morgan Quinn, Sarah Nelson, Alice Berry, Molly Nelson, Robyn Quinn

Mid June I entered into the fifth year of my ministry in Portadown. I have thoroughly enjoyed helping to find photographs and images for this book. The process of illustration and identifying who's who has been a fascinating experience for me. Mervyn Gilmour and all who came up with photographs have indeed enabled me to better get to know my congregation, predecessors and many people I had never met before. Thank you for it.

My hope is that through this illustrated publication of Armagh Road Church history the characters who formed our church activities at different times will come alive again in the images today.

Looking back we can identify God's saints. I am sure you will be able to detect them also ... and perhaps some of them have been an inspiration to you. This is what looking back is all about – to take encouragement and carry dreams forward – those of others and ours also – and realise them in our own lifetime. My prayer for you and me - as we move on:

May the road before us be always in our favour,
may the wind be always at our back;
and until we meet again,
and until we meet again,
may the blessing of God and His grace keep
and surround us.

Christina U. Bradley